A BRIEF HISTORY OF ITALY

TRACING THE RENAISSANCE, UNIFICATION, AND THE LIVELY EVOLUTION OF ART AND CULTURE

DOMINIC HAYNES

CONTENTS

HOW TO GET A FREE SURPRISE HISTORY EBOOK

Get access to the surprise history ebook below and free and unlimited access to all my future books by joining my community.

Scan with your camera to join

INTRODUCTION

Italy. A captivating land bathed in the warm Mediterranean sun that boasts an extraordinary tapestry of history, culture, and innovation. From its ancient roots as the cradle of the Roman Empire to its remarkable Renaissance and beyond, Italy has left an indelible mark on the world, far more significant than the geographical area it occupies. Its cities have witnessed the rise and fall of civilizations, tremendous achievements in art and science, and the triumphs and tribulations of countless generations.

The pages of this book will reveal an enlightening voyage that unveils the captivating story of Italy's past. From the magnificent ruins of Pompeii to the grandeur of Florence's Renaissance masterpieces, the intricate layers of this remarkable nation's history and the forces that have shaped it will be explored.

Meet the early Etruscans, who established the foundations of Italian civilization, the mighty Roman Empire, which ruled over vast territories, and learn about the seismic impact of the Dark Ages that followed. Bear witness to the rise of formidable city-states, such as Venice and Genoa, which became influential hubs of trade and innovation. Fall in love with the groundbreaking artistry of Leonardo da Vinci, Michelangelo Buonarroti, and the other luminaries of the Renaissance, whose genius not only transformed Italy but also reverberated throughout the world.

Moreover, gaze beyond the famous names and iconic landmarks. Peek into the lives of ordinary Italians and hear of their struggles, triumphs, and contributions to the nation's history. Look to the profound influence of the Catholic Church and the papacy, the fervor of the Italian Risorgimento that led to unification, and the challenges faced by Italy in the modern era.

Discover how this great nation has been a crucible of art, philosophy, science, and political intrigue for millennia and continues to be a source of influence and attraction in the modern age.

1

PRELUDE TO EMPIRE: ANCIENT ITALY'S DIVERSE CIVILIZATIONS (3200–90 BCE)

Tucked between the Alps to the north and the beginning of the Apennine mountain range to the south lies the fertile Po River Valley. Also known as the Padan Plain, this rolling green land is perfect for agriculture. Much like the Yellow River, Indus River, or the Tigris and Euphrates Rivers that birthed mighty ancient civilizations, the Po River Valley provides an ideal environment for human settlement. Around 850,000 years ago, as the Po River Valley emerged—it was previously underwater—early humans began to arrive in Italy. Archaeologists posit that the region became an escape for hominids looking for a more moderate climate since the earth was colder and drier at that time.

With the longest river in Italy, the Po River Valley became home to the earliest Italians. Their traces have been discovered at the Ca' Belvedere site in Monte Poggiolo, roughly 10 miles (16 kilometers) outside the town of Forli. Agricultural communities emerged in the Po River Valley during the Neolithic period (10000 BCE–2200 BCE). These early settlers cultivated crops and raised livestock. Their villages were often situated near rivers and lakes, exploiting the fertile soil and abundant water sources.

As the world entered the Copper Age or Chalcolithic Period (c. 3200–2300 BCE), the existence of several civilizations in the Italian peninsula can be established. Not much is known of these early peoples, and their names are derived mainly from the locations where archaeologists discovered the remains of their culture. Mostly, they are remembered for their consistent use of copper, hence the name of the period. Utilizing metal in humanity's tools made farming more efficient, enabling the support of larger family groups. One of the most famous Copper Age discoveries is Ötzi the Iceman, Europe's oldest mummy. Accidentally preserved in the ice of the Alps, he was discovered by a group of hikers in 1991 on the Val Senales Glacier. Older than the pyramids of Egypt and Stonehenge, his corpse and the items found with him have offered valuable clues into the daily life of Copper Age peoples.

One of these enigmatic Chalcolithic groups is the Remedello culture. Discovered in northern Italy in the 1800s CE near the small town of Remedello in Lombardy, they are mainly noted for their funerary practices. Found buried in either crouched positions on their side or flat on their backs, the discovery of the Remedello necropolis hints at the development of a societal warrior class. Not every being found on the site was buried with artifacts, but those that were were mostly male, and the items found in their burial sites were copper and stone weapons.

The Copper Age's end and the Bronze Age's (c. 3000–1000 BCE) dawn are often muddled, with different civilizations gaining bronze metalworking technology at different times. Although thinking of history in neatly divided chunks is tempting, the reality is often far less clear-cut. The beginnings and ends of various eras are blurry and unclear because change is gradual. It is hard to nail down a precise date that the Copper Age became the Bronze Age. Nevertheless, some of Italy's notable Bronze Age societies are the Nuragic civilization on the island of Sardinia and the Terramare culture.

The Nuragic civilization thrived on the island of Sardinia, located in the Mediterranean Sea west of the Italian mainland. This civilization developed during the

Bronze Age and existed from around 1800 BCE to 238 BCE, with its peak period occurring between 1500 BCE and 1200 BCE.

The name "Nuragic" comes from the characteristic archaeological structures called nuraghes. Nuraghes are stone towers built by the Nuragic people and are one of the most distinctive features of their civilization. These towers were likely used for various purposes, including defensive fortifications, religious rituals, and symbols of power.

The Nuragic civilization was organized into a complex network of settlements consisting of villages, towns, and city-states. They were skilled in metalworking, mainly in bronze, and produced intricate bronze objects such as weapons, tools, and statues. The Nuragic people also engaged in agriculture, herding, and maritime activities, including trading with other Mediterranean cultures.

The Nuragic civilization declined around the 2nd century BCE due to various factors, including outside influences and the expansion of the Roman Empire. The Roman conquest of Sardinia led to the assimilation of the Nuragic people into the broader Roman culture.

Back in the Po River Valley, the Terramare culture was flourishing, particularly in the regions of Emilia-

Romagna and Lombardy. The term "Terramare" derives from the Italian words "terra" (earth) and "mare" (sea) and refers to the characteristic land and water features of their settlements. The Terramare people live in the archeological record from 1700 BCE to 1150 BCE.

Primarily small villages consisting of wooden huts built on wooden stilts, these settlements were located on artificially raised mounds called terramare, which were constructed using layers of clay, soil, and wooden platforms. Like their other contemporaneous Bronze Age societies, the Terramare fed themselves via agriculture, cultivating crops such as wheat, barley, millet, and legumes. They also raised livestock, including cattle, pigs, and sheep. Fishing and hunting likely supplemented their food resources.

The decline of the Terramare civilization is thought to have been caused by a combination of factors, including environmental changes, internal conflicts, and invasions from other cultures. It has also been posited that the Terramare were the elusive "Sea Peoples" who wreaked havoc on the Mediterranean region towards the end of the Bronze Age and precipitated a tremendous societal upheaval and collapse. As a side note, the rise of the Villanovan culture marked the transition from the Terramare civilization to the Iron Age in the region. Archaeological excavations at various

Terramare sites, such as Castellazzo di Fontanellato and Montale, have provided valuable insights into this ancient civilization's way of life, technology, and social structure.

As the Bronze Age gradually declined, the earliest migrations of the Italic tribes began to arrive. Part of a larger Indo-European migratory movement around the 2nd millennium BCE, they migrated from the north and settled in various parts of the Italian Peninsula. Among the prominent Italic tribes were the Latins, Sabines, Samnites, Umbrians, and Oscans, each with their own distinct cultural and linguistic characteristics, though they did have certain cultural-linguistic commonalities. These tribes left a deep mark on Italy's cultural and linguistic landscape and continue to be relevant to the region's history.

The Latins, who settled in the area around Rome, played a crucial role in the development of Roman civilization. The city of Rome itself was originally a small village established by Latin settlers on the banks of the Tiber River. Over time, Rome grew into a powerful city-state and eventually the center of the Roman Empire, leaving an enduring mark on the world—but more on that later.

The Sabines, another influential Italic tribe, settled in central Italy. They established various city-states, such as

Amiternum and Nursia, and contributed to the cultural and political environment of the region. The Sabines were known for their military prowess and were often in conflict with the neighboring Latins. This was enshrined in Roman lore by the ancient historian Livy who relayed a tale of Romulus (the mythical founder of Rome) and his troops kidnapping a large number of Sabine women during a conflict between the tribes. This incident, alternatively referred to as the rape of the Sabine women, has been immortalized by prolific painters such as Jacques-Louis David, Nicholas Poussin, Peter Paul Rubens, Edgar Degas, and most recently, Pablo Picasso.

The Samnites inhabited the mountainous regions of southern Italy, primarily in the Apennine Mountains, and were likely an offshoot of the Sabine tribe. They were fierce warriors and fought several conflicts with the Romans during the Samnite Wars (341–290 BCE). Despite their eventual defeat, the Samnites left a lasting impact on the development of Roman military tactics and society.

The Umbrians settled in central Italy, primarily in the region known as Umbria. They were not considered particularly warlike and, unlike the Sabines and Samnites, fought no major wars against the Romans. The Oscans, another Italic tribe, occupied parts of southern Italy, including Campania and Lucania.

It is important to note that the concept of Italian identity as we understand it today did not exist during the time of the Italic tribes. The Italic tribes were diverse, each with their cultural practices and languages. A more cohesive Italian identity began to form over time through the subsequent interactions, conflicts, and assimilation with other peoples, such as the Greeks and Etruscans.

Though the incursions of the Italic tribes and their Indo-European heritage changed the landscape of Italy, there were still native groups and languages that survived in the Iron Age (c. 1200–600 BCE). One such group is the Villanovan culture, an ancient civilization that thrived in central and northern Italy from approximately the 9th century BCE to the 7th century BCE. It was named after the village of Villanova, near Bologna, where the culture was first identified through archaeological excavations.

Perhaps it was the influence of new people in the area or just the result of humankind's natural progress, but the Villanovan culture marked a significant alteration in the region's social and cultural composition. From the organization of their communities to their technological and artistic developments, the evidence unearthed in archaeological excavations has offered a fascinating insight into the transition from the Bronze Age to the Iron Age.

Villanovan communities consisted of small agricultural villages, often fortified with defensive walls. The society was organized into clan-based groups, with kinship playing a crucial role in social structure. The villages typically had central communal areas, burials, and workshops.

Known for their advanced ironworking techniques, which significantly impacted their material culture, Villanovans swapped bronze for iron as the primary metal for tools, weapons, and ornaments. The mastery of ironworking contributed to the military power and economic prosperity of the Villanovan culture.

Furthermore, Villanovan burials are among the most striking aspects of the culture. They constructed elaborate burial mounds, known as *tumuli*, which contained grave goods such as pottery vessels, weapons, jewelry, and personal items. These grave goods reflect the social status and wealth of the individuals buried within. The pottery discovered in these *tumuli* is distinct, featuring geometric designs, incised decorations, and biconical shapes. The pottery often had dark burnished surfaces, with some examples featuring intricate patterns and stylized animal motifs.

The Villanovan culture eventually gave way to the Etruscan civilization, which profoundly influenced the development of ancient Italy. Some also argue that the Villanovans were simply an early version of the Etruscan people. The Etruscans inherited and expanded upon many aspects of Villanovan culture, including their ironworking techniques, art styles, and burial practices.

Even to those with minimal knowledge of Italian history, the importance of the Roman civilization looms large. However, before the Romans came the Etruscans, and without their influence and culture, it is possible that Rome would never have risen to the heights it achieved.

The Etruscans were an ancient civilization that flourished in central Italy, primarily in the region known as Etruria (present-day Tuscany, western Umbria, and northern Lazio), from approximately the 8th century BCE to the 3rd century BCE. As mentioned above, they were critical in shaping the development of Italy and influenced the early Romans. Roman culture, society, and governance can find roots in the Etruscan way of life. Etruscan kings even ruled over Rome for some time before the Roman Republic was established.

The origins of the Etruscans are still debated among scholars. While, as mentioned earlier, many believe they emerged from the indigenous Villanovan peoples, they likely also had influences from other Mediterranean cultures. What is known is that the Etruscans were skilled traders and seafarers. They established a network of trade routes that connected them with various Mediterranean civilizations, including the Greeks and Phoenicians. The Etruscans acquired luxury goods, such as ceramics, metals, and precious stones, through extensive trade contacts, influencing their art and culture.

The Etruscan language, which is not closely related to any other known language, was deciphered to some extent but remains only partially understood. As for its relationship with Latin, the two are from different language families, with Latin descending from an Indo-European root, like Greek, Sanskrit, and the various Celtic dialects. On the other hand, Etruscan has no known linguistic relatives.

However, it likely influenced Vulgar Latin (the spoken form of Latin) due to the two cultures' proximity and interrelations. There was one massive influence, though—the Etruscan alphabet. The Romans acquired their early alphabet from the Etruscans, who, in turn, had adopted it from the Greek alphabet. The Latin alphabet, as used by the Romans, was derived from the Etruscan variant with some modifications. The

Etruscan influence on the development of the Latin script laid the foundation for the written language that became widely used in ancient Rome and eventually evolved into modern Western alphabets. The Romans also adopted Etruscan legal concepts, such as the idea of written laws and the appointment of judges.

The Etruscan society was organized into several independent city-states, the most notable being Veii, Tarquinia, Vulci, and Cerveteri. These city-states had their own rulers—lucumones—and often engaged in rivalries and alliances. Etruscan society had a hierarchical structure, with aristocratic elites holding significant power. Etruscan society exhibited some unique social customs and practices. Women held relatively high status and enjoyed greater freedoms than their contemporaries in other ancient civilizations. Etruscan women participated in public life, attended banquets, and were depicted in artwork alongside men. Etruscan women also played a role in religious ceremonies and were sometimes buried with their own grave goods.

Known for their engineering prowess, they constructed impressive systems of roads, bridges, and drainage networks that facilitated trade and communication. They also built advanced hydraulic engineering works, including canals and tunnels, allowing efficient irrigation and water management in their agricultural lands.

Etruscan urban planning and architectural styles had a noticeable impact on the Romans. Etruscan cities were organized on grid patterns, and their architectural elements, such as arches, vaults, and drainage systems, influenced Roman city planning and engineering practices. Etruscan temple designs and architectural motifs also found their way into Roman architecture.

Beyond their architectural abilities, the Etruscans were also renowned for their artistic achievements. They excelled in metalworking, producing intricate gold jewelry, bronze statues, and decorative items. Their beautiful artistry extended into their fashion sense, and the Romans adopted certain clothing styles and fashion trends from the Etruscans. Etruscan influence can be seen in the Roman use of draped garments, as well as the use of specific types of jewelry, hairstyles, and accessories. Etruscan artistic representations of fashion and personal adornment influenced Roman artistic and sartorial traditions.

Etruscan tomb paintings depicted scenes from daily life, mythology, and funerary rituals. The origins of the gladiatorial games, a distinctive aspect of Roman entertainment, can be traced back to Etruscan funeral rituals. The Etruscans conducted funeral games and combats as part of their funeral customs, and the Romans later adopted and transformed these practices into the gladiatorial spectacles that became popular in Roman society. They also constructed impressive monumental architecture, such as temples, tombs, and city walls. The survival of these tombs and temples has shown what a vital role religion played in Etruscan society. Their elaborate underground tombs, often referred to as necropolises, contained multiple chambers for the deceased and their grave goods. These tombs were adorned with frescoes and housed various items reflecting the individual's status and beliefs.

A complex system of religious beliefs and various deities was associated with many aspects of life. Etruscans believed that their gods significantly influenced their human affairs and practiced haruspicy, the examination of animal entrails, as an important form of divination in their religious rituals. The Romans adopted several religious beliefs and practices from the Etruscans, particularly their fascination with divination and augury, the interpretation of signs and omens from the gods. The Romans incorporated Etruscan divination techniques into their religious rituals, such as examining haruspicy and interpreting lightning strikes (fulguration).

The decline of the Etruscan civilization began in the 4th century BCE due to a combination of factors, including territorial conflicts, invasions, and Roman expansion. By the 3rd century BCE, the region of Etruria was absorbed into the Roman Republic. Etruscan culture gradually assimilated into the broader Roman society, fully incorporating the culture into Rome by 90 BCE. The Etruscan language ceased to be spoken and was eventually replaced by Latin. Many Etruscan cities and their architectural wonders were gradually abandoned or repurposed. Nevertheless, Etruscan art, pottery, and craftsmanship continued to influence Roman art and culture, leaving a lasting impact on the development of ancient Italy.

Our understanding of the Etruscans relies heavily on archaeological discoveries, including tomb excavations, inscriptions, artifacts, and accounts from Greek and Roman sources. However, many aspects of their culture and history remain mysterious and subject to ongoing research and exploration.

As the Etruscans built their society in Etruria, another invading population entered Italy. The Greek colonization of ancient Italy, occurring from the 8th century BCE onward, marked a notable period of expansion and cultural exchange. The Greek city-states were driven by a desire for new trade routes, agricultural resources, and fertile land, and established colonies along Italy's southern and western coasts. This colonization wave, known as the Greek expansion, brought the Greek language, culture, and political structures to Italian shores.

Small groups of settlers from various Greek city-states founded Greek colonies in Italy. These pioneers sought to establish independent city-states that mirrored their homeland's political and social structures. Prominent Greek colonies, such as Sybaris, Croton, Tarentum (Taranto), and Neapolis (Naples), emerged as centers of Greek influence in Italy. They flourished economically, benefiting from the fertile land and strategic coastal locations. Engaging in maritime trade, they exported agricultural products, ceramics, and other goods. The colonies played a pivotal role in expanding Greek influence throughout the Mediterranean, contributing to a vibrant economic network in the region.

These settlements introduced the Greek language, art, and religious practices to the Italian peninsula. They implemented Greek-style city planning and agriculture techniques and constructed impressive temples and theaters. The interaction between Greek settlers, Etruscans, and the Italic tribes resulted in cultural exchange and the assimilation of Greek customs into local traditions. However, the relationship between the Greek colonizers and the inhabitants of the Italian peninsula was not all friendly. Though many encounters between the Etruscans and the Italic tribes were peaceful trade negotiations, territorial disputes and occasional conflicts arose. The Greek colonies often faced competition and hostilities from rival powers, notably the Etruscans and the rising Roman Republic.

In the end, though Greek colonization resulted in the diffusion of Greek culture throughout the Mediterranean, as the Roman Republic expanded its control over Italy, many Greek colonies were eventually assimilated into Roman territories. However, the influence of Greek culture on the region cannot be ignored, as it influenced Rome and, later, the nation of Italy.

In the millennia preceding the rise of the mighty Roman Empire, the Italian peninsula was a vibrant tapestry of ancient civilizations. From the mysterious Etruscans to the influential Greeks, the land of Italy bore witness to a rich mosaic of cultures, each leaving its undeniable mark on the region's history.

The Etruscans dominated central Italy with their advanced agricultural practices, remarkable craftsmanship, and intricate religious beliefs. Their city-states flourished, boasting impressive architecture, elaborate tombs, and a society where women enjoyed unprecedented rights and social standing.

To the south, Greek colonies thrived along the coastline, transforming Italy into a hub of trade and cultural exchange. The Greeks brought their language, literature, philosophy, and artistic traditions, shaping the intellectual landscape of the peninsula. Greek colonies, like Neapolis and Tarentum, became beacons of Hellenic civilization, fostering economic prosperity and connections with the wider Mediterranean world.

Meanwhile, the Italic peoples, such as the Samnites and Umbrians, inhabited Italy's rugged and diverse regions. These ancient tribes possessed their own distinct cultures, customs, and intricate social structures. They cultivated the land, constructed impressive fortified settlements, and engaged in peaceful trade and occasional conflicts with their neighbors.

As these ancient civilizations coexisted and interacted, the Italian peninsula became a dynamic and ever-evolving river of cultural fusion. It was a place where ideas, traditions, and goods flowed, influencing one another and leaving a lasting impact on the collective identity of Italy.

Yet, amidst this vibrant tapestry, a new power emerged that would eventually unite and dominate the entire peninsula—the Romans. Their rise to power and the subsequent transformation of Italy would forever change the course of history, shaping the region's destiny and leaving an enduring legacy that resonates today.

As we turn the page to the next chapter, we delve into the fascinating story of Rome's ascent and its profound impact on Italy, tracing the path of an empire that would define the ancient world.

2

DOMINION OF THE EAGLES: THE ROMAN ERA IN ITALY (753 BCE–476 CE)

According to legend and myth, the founding of Rome is attributed to Romulus and Remus, twin brothers who were said to have been raised by a she-wolf. The story goes that the brothers were descendants of the Trojan hero Aeneas, who fled from Troy after its fall and eventually arrived on the Italian peninsula.

The story of Romulus and Remus has varying forms, but here is the general plotline. As the twins grew older, they decided to establish a city of their own. However, a dispute arose between them over the choice of location. Romulus endorsed the Palatine Hill, while Remus desired the Aventine Hill. Unable to resolve their differences, they sought divine intervention.

Legend has it that they obtained guidance from the gods by observing the flight of birds. Remus claimed to have seen six birds first, while Romulus later reported seeing twelve. Believing that the gods favored him, Romulus proceeded to mark the boundaries of his chosen hill by plowing a furrow around it, symbolizing the walls of the future city.

Remus leaped over the furrow, seemingly mocking his brother's efforts. Angered by this defiance, Romulus killed Remus, thus securing his claim as the sole founder of the city. He named the new settlement "Roma" after himself, and it is said to have been founded on April 21, 753 BCE.

While the founding of Rome is steeped in mythology and legend, historical records suggest that the city gradually developed through urbanization and the integration of various neighboring communities. Over time, Rome grew in size and significance, eventually evolving into the capital of a vast empire that would leave an enduring mark on the world.

There are several recognized periods of Roman history: The Regal Period, the Roman Republic, and the Roman Empire. The Regal Period of Rome refers to the time of the Roman monarchy. It is the earliest phase of Rome's history and is believed to have lasted from approximately 753 BCE to 509 BCE.

According to traditional accounts, seven legendary kings ruled Rome during this period. These kings are as follows: Romulus (r. 753–716 BCE), Numa Pompilius (r. 715–673 BCE), Tullus Hostilius (r. 673–642 BCE), Ancus Marcius (r. 642–617 BCE), Tarquinius Priscus (r. 616–579 BCE), Servius Tullius (r. 578–535 BCE), and Tarquinius Superbus (r. 534–509 BCE). Each king offered something to the foundation of Rome, though the veracity of these legends is quite unclear.

As the city's legendary founder, Romulus established the framework for the early Roman state and its institutions. He also organized the population into military units known as legions. His successor, Numa Pompilius, was known for his religious reforms and establishment of various institutions for the faithful. He is credited with creating the calendar and promoting peace and the arts. Tullus Hostilius, on the other hand, was known as a warlike king who expanded Rome's territory and military power. He is often associated with the conflict between Rome and the ancient neighboring city of Alba Longa.

Ancus Marcius turned his focus inward, honing in on the development of Rome's infrastructure and the expansion of the city. He constructed various public buildings, such as the first bridge across the Tiber River. Tarquinius Priscus was believed to be an

Etruscan king who introduced several innovations to Rome, including the construction of the Circus Maximus (a home for chariot racing and gladiator games) and the expansion of the Roman Senate. Though his successor, Servius Tullius, continued Tarquinius Priscus' political reforms, he also introduced some adjustments to the Roman military. Best remembered for establishing the Servian Constitution, which organized Roman society into classes based on wealth, Servius Tullius was allegedly responsible for the general structure of Roman society. Finally came Tarquinius Superbus, also known as Tarquin the Proud, the last king of Rome. His rule was marked by tyranny and oppressive governance, leading to the revolt of the Roman people, which ultimately resulted in the establishment of the Roman Republic.

Remember that the historicity of the Regal Period and the details of the reigns of these kings are subject to debate and often liberally blend history with mythology and legend. However, these legendary figures and their stories played a crucial role in shaping Rome's early identity and foundation, and there is likely some truth to their existence and accomplishments.

The founding of the Roman Republic marks a significant turning point in Roman history: the transition from monarchical rule to a system of government based on shared power and representation. As mentioned earlier, the traditional account of the establishment of the Republic is attributed to the overthrow of the last Roman king, Tarquinius Superbus, in 509 BCE.

According to legend, Tarquinius Superbus and his family ruled Rome with tyranny and oppression, which led to growing discontent among the Roman people. The catalyst for the revolution was the rape of Lucretia, a noblewoman, by Tarquinius' son. This heinous act outraged the Roman aristocracy, and they rose up against the oppressive rule of the Tarquin family.

Lucius Junius Brutus, a prominent Roman noble, played a central role in leading the revolt against the monarchy. He rallied the Roman people's support and gained the Senate's trust. Together with Lucius Tarquinius Collatinus, the husband of Lucretia, they formed a coalition to oust the Tarquin family and establish a new system of government.

The Romans declared themselves a republic, with Brutus and Collatinus serving as the first consuls. The consuls were established as elected officials who held executive and military powers. Responsible for leading the state, executing laws, and commanding the military, the rise of the consuls and the formation of the Republic also marked the end of hereditary kingship and the introduction of term limits for elected officials.

Based on the principle of *res publica*, meaning "public affair" or "commonwealth," the Roman Republic aimed to distribute power among different institutions and prevent the concentration of authority in a single individual or family. The Republic was governed by a system of checks and balances, which included the Senate, assemblies, and magistrates. The Senate, composed of influential and experienced individuals, served as an advisory and legislative body. Meanwhile, the assemblies provided a platform for Roman citizens to participate in decision-making, vote on laws, and elect officials. Lastly, various magistrates were appointed to enforce laws and administer justice.

The founding of the Roman Republic marked a new era in Roman history, characterized by a more inclusive and participatory form of government. The five centuries that it endured from 509 to 27 BCE saw a time of political, social, and military transformations that shaped the destiny of Rome and laid the foundation for its later empire. Though massive tomes could be written about many of the events that occurred throughout Rome's existence, note that this text will only briefly scratch the surface to offer all the salient points about Italy's vast history.

Even though the Republic offered a more equitable governing solution for its people than the monarchy, this did not mean class struggles and conflicts evaporated. The Republic's early days saw the Conflict of the Orders, spanning from 494 to 287 BCE. It was a pivotal struggle within the Roman Republic between the patricians (aristocratic class) and the plebeians (common citizens). The plebeians, facing economic hardships and political marginalization, fought for greater representation and protection of their rights. Through persistent efforts, they gained concessions, such as the creation of the Tribune of the Plebs, a position that allowed plebeians to veto legislation and protect their interests. Over time, the Conflict of the Orders led to greater social and political equality, as the plebeians secured the ability to participate in the Republic's decision-making processes, challenging the patrician elite's dominance.

Conflict also swelled abroad between the Romans and their various neighbors. Driven by a desire for security and resources, Rome embarked on a path of territorial expansion. The Republic engaged in a series of wars, including the Samnite Wars (343–c. 295 BCE) and the Pyrrhic War (280–275 BCE), through which it gradually expanded its dominion over the Italian peninsula.

With their homeland largely subdued, the Romans turned their eyes abroad, particularly to the powerful maritime civilization of Carthage. Founded by the Phoenicians, this ancient culture rivaled Rome in wealth, military might, and cultural influence, leaving an enduring legacy in history. Rome's epic struggles against Carthage, known as the Punic Wars (264–146 BCE), defined the Republic's rivalry with the great North African power. Led by military geniuses such as Scipio Africanus, Rome emerged victorious, securing its dominance in the Mediterranean and gaining new territories.

Beyond Northern Africa, Rome's influence extended eastward with the Macedonian Wars (214–148 BCE) against the Hellenistic Kingdoms. These conflicts, marked by famous battles like Cynoscephalae (197 BCE) and Pydna (168 BCE), led to the Roman conquest of Greece and established its supremacy in the eastern Mediterranean.

Yet, even as Rome amassed more and more territory, conflict continually bubbled within their capital city. The Gracchi brothers, Tiberius and Gaius, were Roman politicians who championed social and economic reforms in the late Republic. Tiberius sought to address land concentration by proposing agrarian reforms, while Gaius aimed for a broader range of reforms, including land redistribution and extending rights to the plebeians. Both faced fierce opposition from the senatorial class, leading to violent confrontations and their eventual deaths. Their efforts to tackle inequality and challenge the power of the elites left a lasting scar on Roman politics, establishing a precedent for pursuing political objectives through radical means and highlighting the growing social tensions within the Republic.

The tragic demise of the Gracchi brothers created a power vacuum in the Roman Republic and heightened the existing political instability. It set the stage for the rise of Julius Caesar, who would emerge as a formidable figure, shaping the course of Roman history and ultimately leading to the transformation of the Republic into an empire.

Born on July 12 or 13, 100 BCE, Julius Caesar was a prominent Roman statesman, military general, and one of the most influential figures in ancient history. As is evident by his massive historical importance, he was a necessary ingredient in the transition from the Roman Republic to the Roman Empire.

Caesar came from a noble family and rose through Roman politics and military ranks with charisma, intelligence, and military acumen. He served as a military commander in various campaigns, including the conquest of Gaul (modern-day France), where he demonstrated exceptional leadership and won consequential military victories. His campaigns in Gaul expanded Rome's territories and brought him immense wealth and popularity among his troops.

Caesar's political career was equally remarkable. To consolidate power, Julius Caesar, Pompey the Great, and Marcus Lincinius Crassus formed a political alliance known as the First Triumvirate. This unofficial partnership allowed them to exert significant influence over Roman politics, but tensions among the triumvirs would eventually lead to conflict.

In 49 BCE, Caesar defied the Roman Senate's orders and crossed the Rubicon River, symbolically starting a civil war against Pompey and the Senate. This marked a point of no return, as it was an open rebellion against the Roman state. Caesar emerged victorious after a series of military campaigns, culminating in the Battle of Pharsalus in 48 BCE.

With his triumph, Caesar assumed absolute power and established himself as a dictator. He implemented numerous reforms to address social and political issues, such as land redistribution, reforming the calendar (introducing the Julian calendar), and granting Roman citizenship to more individuals across the empire.

These reforms aimed to bolster his popularity and consolidate his rule.

However, Caesar's increasing power and ambitions unsettled many senators and aristocrats who feared the erosion of the Republic's traditional institutions. On the Ides of March (March 15), 44 BCE, Caesar was assassinated by a group of senators led by Marcus Junius Brutus and Gaius Cassius Longinus, who believed that his rule threatened Rome's dearly held republican principles.

Julius Caesar's legacy is profound. He is renowned for his military genius, political acumen, and administrative reforms. His life and death marked a turning point in Roman history, leading to the Roman Republic's end and the Roman Empire's rise under Augustus Caesar. Caesar's name became synonymous with the consolidation of power, the shift from republican rule to autocracy, and the beginning of imperial governance in Rome.

This violent assassination of Caesar plunged Rome into chaos. Eventually, it ushered in a power struggle between his supporters, led by Mark Antony, and his assassins, led by Brutus and Cassius. At this time, Gaius Octavius (also known as Octavian), Caesar's adopted heir, emerged as an influential figure in Roman politics. He formed the Second Triumvirate with Antony and

Marcus Aemilius Lepidus, and this struggle between the Triumvirate and Caeser's assassins culminated in the Battle of Philippi in 42 BCE. Antony and Octavian emerged victorious, and together with Lepidus, they divided the Roman world between them.

However, the alliance of the Second Triumvirate eventually dissolved. Lepidus' influence waned, setting up a bitter clash between Octavian and Antony, who had allied himself with the Queen of Egypt, Cleopatra. This all came to a head at the Battle of Actium. Fought on September 2, 31 BCE, Actium was a naval engagement between the forces of Octavian and Antony, with support from his Cleopatra. Octavian triumphed conclusively and secured his position as the sole ruler of Rome. His gain was Antony's loss, as the defeat of Antony and Cleopatra led to their downfall and eventual death. In 27 BCE, he assumed the title of Augustus, marking the end of the Republic and the birth of the Roman Empire. The Republic's prior republican ideals and institutions were gradually transformed into a centralized imperial system.

With the establishment of the Roman Empire under the reign of Augustus Caesar (r. 27 BCE–14 CE), a new era began. Augustus laid the foundation for a stable and centralized imperial government that would endure for centuries. During the early days of the Roman Empire, the principate system was established, with the emperor holding supreme power but still giving the appearance of republican governance. Augustus set a precedent for future emperors, and his successors continued to build Roman authority.

He oversaw the initiation of the *Pax Romana*, or Roman Peace, which is generally considered to have started around the dawn of his rule and lasted until around 180 CE—this period of approximately two centuries witnessed relative peace and stability within the Roman Empire. Characterized by a decline in large-scale military conflicts, the expansion and consolidation of Roman rule, the promotion of trade and economic prosperity, and advancements in art, architecture, and literature, the *Pax Romana* set the stage for the subsequent centuries of Roman dominance.

Following Augustus, the four successive emperors belonged to the Julio-Claudian dynasty. Tiberius (r. 14–37 CE), Caligula (r. 37–41 CE), Claudius (r. 41–54 CE), and Nero (r. 54–68) ruled with varying degrees of success and infamy. The empire experienced relative stability during the reign of Tiberius, but the rules of Caligula and Nero were marked by corruption, extravagance, and cruelty.

After Nero's death by suicide, there was a chaotic interlude before the Flavian Dynasty (69–96 CE) re-established order. Founded by Vespasian (r. 69–79 CE), his reign oversaw a reconstruction of Rome, including the iconic Colosseum, which became a symbol of imperial power and spectacle. His son Titus (r. 79–81 CE) continued his father's legacy, completing the Colosseum and demonstrating capable leadership during the eruption of Mount Vesuvius. However, it was Domitian (r. 81–96), the younger brother of Titus, whose reign displayed a more autocratic style. Despite his accomplishments in military campaigns and infrastructure projects, Domitian's authoritarian rule sparked discontent, leading to his ultimate assassination.

The early empire was a time of outstanding advancements in art, literature, and architecture. Roman culture flourished, with poets like Virgil and Ovid, historians like Tacitus, and architects like Vitruvius leaving lasting contributions. Monumental structures, like the Colosseum, were built, showcasing the engineering and architectural prowess of the empire.

After the reigns of the Julio-Claudian and Flavian dynasties, Rome entered a period of critical political and social changes. This period, often called the "Adoptive Emperors" or the "Five Good Emperors," spanned from the late 1st century CE to the early 2nd century CE.

The Adoptive Emperors, namely Nerva (r. 96–98 CE), Trajan (r. 98–117 CE), Hadrian (r. 117–138 CE), Antoninus Pius (r. 138–161 CE), and Marcus Aurelius (r. 161–180 CE), were known for their successful governance and the peaceful transfer of power through adoption. They prioritized the welfare of the empire, improved administration, and implemented policies aimed at benefiting the populace. This era was characterized by relative stability, economic prosperity, and territorial expansion.

Trajan, in particular, led the empire to its greatest territorial extent, encompassing vast regions of Europe, North Africa, and the Middle East. His expansions led Rome to the zenith of its size with conquests that included the annexation of Dacia (modern-day Romania) and the capture of the prosperous city of Petra in Arabia. As a result, the Roman Empire controlled a diverse array of peoples and cultures, fostering a rich cultural exchange and influencing various aspects of governance, law, language, and architecture.

Hadrian, known for his extensive travels throughout the empire, focused on consolidating and fortifying the frontiers. He initiated the construction of Hadrian's Wall in Britain, which marked the northern limit of the

Roman Empire, and implemented defensive measures to secure the borders.

As a natural consequence of its territorial gains, Rome enjoyed economic growth driven by trade, agriculture, and the exploitation of natural resources. The empire became the premiere center of commerce and wealth, brimming with bustling cities and flourishing industries. Construction of grand public works and monumental buildings, such as the Pantheon and Trajan's Forum, showcased the empire's architectural prowess and opulence. The intellectual and cultural scene also thrived with publications from prominent writers and thinkers such as Epictetus, Pliny the Younger, Juvenal, and the emperor Marcus Aurelius himself, reflecting the philosophical and moral ideals of the time.

The height of the Roman Empire is generally considered to have occurred during the time of the Five Good Emperors, particularly under the reign of Emperor Trajan. This Golden Age is often referred to as the "High Roman Empire," and it marked the pinnacle of Rome's territorial extent, military power, and cultural influence.

However, the height of the Roman Empire was not devoid of challenges and internal tensions. As the empire expanded, it faced increasing pressures and strains on governance, economy, and military resources. While the 2nd century CE represented a time of remarkable achievements, it also foreshadowed the complexities and eventual decline the Roman Empire would face in the centuries to come. The specters of succession, border defense (particularly against the Germanic tribes), economic pressures, social cohesion, corruption, and conflict from within haunted the time of the Five Good Emperors and would only grow as the years passed.

After the death of Marcus Aurelius, the reign of his son, Commodus (r. 180–192 CE), proved tyrannical and ineffective. Here began the slow, painful downward spiral of the Roman Empire. While pinpointing a single cause for the decline is complex, various factors contributed to its gradual unraveling. Commodus, known for his extravagant lifestyle and despotic rule, marked the beginning of a series of weak and ineffective emperors who were bedeviled by military coups, civil wars, and various political upheavals. Their mismanagement of the empire's affairs, rampant corruption, and self-serving policies eroded the stability and integrity of the state. The deterioration of the political system resulted in frequent assassinations, civil wars, and a decline in effective governance.

External threats also posed significant challenges to the empire. Germanic invasions from the north, particularly by the Visigoths, Ostrogoths, Vandals, and other tribes, put pressure on the frontiers and weakened the empire's defenses. Concurrently, the Sassanid Empire in the east proved to be a formidable rival, leading to conflicts and territorial losses for Rome.

Economic troubles plagued the empire as well. Inflation, debasement of the currency, and financial mismanagement caused economic instability. The reliance on slave labor and the decline of small-scale farming disrupted the rural economy, leading to social unrest and a growing divide between the wealthy elite and the impoverished masses.

Internal divisions and the loss of a unified sense of identity also played a role in the empire's downfall. The spread of Christianity, while offering solace to many, weakened traditional Roman religious and cultural beliefs. The increasing fragmentation of the empire into separate regions with their own aspirations and loyalties further eroded the unity that had once sustained Rome.

By the 5th century CE, the Western Roman Empire faced continued invasions, political fragmentation, and a lack of effective central authority. In 476 CE, the last Roman emperor, tragically and poetically named Romulus Augustus (r. 475–476 CE), was deposed by Odoacer, a Germanic chieftain, marking the end of the

Western Roman Empire. Though the Eastern Roman Empire, now known as the Byzantine Empire, would continue until its seat in Constantinople was sacked by the Ottoman Empire in 1453 CE, the Rome of Romulus, Julius Caesar, and Caesar Augustus faded into the mists of time. The eagle, the telltale standard of the Roman Legion, flew no more.

As this chapter on Rome closes, all that remains is a profound appreciation for its enduring impact on Italian history and the world at large. From its humble origins as a small village to its rise as a mighty empire, Rome enjoys an enduring legacy in politics, law, architecture, literature, and culture. It has been a beacon of power and a crucible of civilization, showcasing both the heights of human achievement and the depths of human frailty. The story of Rome is one of triumph and tragedy, grandeur and decline, but through it all, the Eternal City has remained a symbol of resilience and timeless fascination. The lessons and legacy of Rome are a high point in the annals of Italian history, forever shaping the understanding of the past and informing the aspirations for the future.

3

A SPLINTERED LEGACY: ITALY AFTER THE FALL (476–1100 CE)

The resounding echoes of a once-great empire faded away, leaving behind a shattered mosaic of political upheaval, cultural transformation, and uncertain futures. Once the crown jewel of the Roman Empire, Italy stood as a fragmented land, its majestic cities bearing witness to the ebb and flow of conquerors and conquerors-to-be. With the demise of the Western Roman Empire in 476 CE, the stage was set for a tumultuous era that would shape the destiny of Italy and reverberate across the ages. As the dust settled and the shadow of Rome began to wane, a vivid tapestry of kingdoms, republics, and empires emerged, each vying for supremacy in a land teeming with rich history and relentless spirit.

Though the previous chapter primarily focused on the legacy of the Western Roman Empire, for clarity's sake, it is important to take a moment to rehash the fate of the Eastern Roman Empire. By the 3rd century CE, the Roman Empire had become too vast to be effectively governed from a single center. As a result, the empire was divided administratively into two parts: the Western Roman Empire, with its capital in Rome, and the Eastern Roman Empire, with its capital in Byzantium (later known as Constantinople).

As previously noted, the decline of the Roman Empire in the West was marked by a series of internal conflicts, external invasions, economic challenges, and administrative problems. Emperor Diocletian (r. 284–305 CE) attempted to stabilize the empire in the late 3rd and early 4th centuries CE. He introduced administrative reforms, including the division of power and the establishment of the Tetrarchy, which involved the appointment of two Augusti (senior emperors) and two Caesars (junior emperors) to govern different regions of the empire. This division set the stage for the eventual split between East and West.

Emperor Constantine the Great, who ruled from 306 to 337 CE, played a crucial role in the split. He established Byzantium as his new capital, which he renamed

Constantinople (present-day Istanbul). This signaled a shift in power and influence toward the eastern regions of the empire. The Theodosian Dynasty, particularly Emperor Theodosius I (r. East 379–392 CE, East and West 392–395 CE), further solidified the division between East and West. The empire was officially divided into two separate entities in 395 CE after Theodosius' death, with his sons Arcadius ruling the East and Honorius the West.

Over time, the Eastern and Western Roman Empires developed distinct cultural and religious identities. The Eastern Empire, also known as the Byzantine Empire, had a predominantly Greek-speaking population and was heavily influenced by Greek and Eastern traditions. In contrast, the Western Empire, centered in Rome, maintained its Latin language and customs. The two also had differing theologies, with Catholics in the West answering to the pope in Rome and Orthodox Christians in the East beholden to the patriarch in Constantinople.

The influence of Roman authority on these two religious figures would direct European history for the next several centuries. In the West, there was no strong ruler (particularly after 476 CE) to check the increasing power of the papacy. As a result, many of the ensuing centuries in Europe revolved around which entities should ultimately have more power: the pope or the kings. In the Eastern Roman Empire, however, the emperor appointed the patriarch directly, making it clear who was in charge. This practice is referred to as "caesaropapism," or the practice of placing the secular offices above and in charge of religious ones.

First to rise from the ashes of the Western Roman Empire were the very people responsible for the final nail in its coffin: the Germanic tribes. In 476 CE, Odoacer, a Germanic chieftain and military leader of the Heruli, Sciri, and Rugii, led a revolt against the last Western Roman Emperor, Romulus Augustus. Odoacer deposed him, bringing an end to the Western Roman Empire. This event is often considered the official end of the ancient Roman Empire.

After the deposition of Romulus Augustus, Odoacer did not declare himself emperor. Instead, he sought recognition and legitimacy from the Eastern Roman Emperor, Zeno (r. 474–491 CE). In 480 CE, Zeno appointed Odoacer as the patrician and ruler of Italy, acknowledging his authority. In doing so, Odoacer became the first barbarian king of Italy. He maintained a relatively amicable relationship with the Eastern Roman Empire at first. He recognized the nominal suzerainty of the Eastern Roman Emperor and sent regular payments as a sign of loyalty. However, Odoacer effectively ruled Italy as an independent kingdom, making his own decisions regarding internal affairs.

A combination of Germanic military leadership and Roman administrative structures characterized his rule in Italy. Still, he kept a lot of the original framework of Imperial Rome in place. He adopted a policy of maintaining Roman governmental institutions and legal systems. Odoacer allowed prominent Roman aristocrats to retain their positions in government. Many of the established elite continued to hold administrative roles and seats of power. Mainly, he sought to maintain a sense of continuity and reinforce his legitimacy by incorporating Rome's essence into his rule.

Odoacer's reign faced challenges from other Germanic tribes, particularly the Ostrogoths led by Theodoric the Great. Theodoric had been a thorn in the side of the Byzantine Emperor Zeno for some time. Aware of his military prowess, Zeno had named Theodoric Master of Soldiers in 483 CE. However, unsatisfied with the rewards bestowed on him for protecting the Byzantine Empire from outside invaders, he began a campaign against Zeno, raiding and pillaging the lands he had once protected.

It is unknown which party—Zeno or Theodoric—suggested that he overthrow Odoacer, but sometime around 488 CE, Theodoric initiated a campaign to conquer Italy with Zeno's support. After all, Zeno, though he had initially approved of Odoacer's kingship, had soured on the monarch over time since Odoacer had caused problems for the empire by acting increasingly independent of Zeno's control. At last, in 493 CE, after years of conflict, Theodoric finally defeated and subsequently killed Odoacer. Thus the peninsula fell into new hands, establishing the Ostrogothic Kingdom in Italy.

However, despite the leadership change, it was very much a case of "Meet the new boss, same as the old boss." Like Odoacer, Theodoric sought to maintain Roman administrative structures and promote stability in Italy. He respected Roman traditions, laws, and institutions and often presented himself as a defender of Roman culture. Theodoric implemented a well-organized administration that combined Gothic and Roman elements. He appointed Roman senators and bureaucrats alongside Gothic officials, fostering a sense of integration.

Theodoric's court became a center of cultural patronage. He encouraged the restoration of public buildings, aqueducts, and monuments, contributing to the preservation of Roman heritage. Theodoric attracted notable scholars and intellectuals, creating a climate of learning and intellectual exchange.

Religious tolerance was also a central aspect of Theodoric's rule. He pursued a policy of religious reconciliation between the Arian Christian Ostrogoths and the Catholic Christian majority in Italy. Theodoric allowed religious freedom and supported the construction and restoration of churches. However, tensions between the Arian Goths and Catholic Romans occasionally led to skirmishes. For all his talk of tolerance, Theodoric favored Arian Christianity over Catholicism, leading to some instances of mistreatment of Catholic bishops and clergy members. It is important to add that Arian Christians were also persecuted within the Byzantine Empire, where Eastern Orthodoxy was the primary form of Christianity.

Religion has not been a prominent topic of discussion thus far, but a brief sidebar is warranted to explain the differences between Arian Christianity and Catholicism. Arianism arose in the early 4th century CE thanks to the work of Arius, a Christian presbyter from Alexandria, Egypt. Arian Christians believe that Jesus Christ, as the Son of God, was created by God the Father and was, therefore, subordinate to the Father. They rejected the concept of the Holy Trinity as co-

equal and consubstantial (of one substance), emphasizing the distinction between the persons of God the
Father and Jesus Christ, his son.

Conversely, Roman Catholics, who trace their identity
and roots back to the earliest Christian communities in
Rome, follow the teachings of the Bible, tradition, and
the authority of the pope, who is considered the
successor of Saint Peter and the head of the Catholic
Church. Unlike the Arians, Catholics believe whole-
heartedly in the doctrine of the Holy Trinity, that is, the
concept that God exists in three persons: God the
Father, God the Son (Jesus), and God the Holy Spirit.
They consider the Father, Son and Holy Spirit to be
consubstantial.

Arianism was considered a heresy by the Catholic
Church, as it contradicted the doctrine of the Holy
Trinity that later became central to Christian belief.
Most Christians in the world today are Trinitarians.
The Arian controversy had significant theological and
political implications, leading to debates, divisions, and
conflicts within the early Christian community.

Over time, Arianism gradually lost influence, especially
after the Council of Nicaea in 325 CE, where the
Christian position was solidified, and Arian doctrines
were rejected. With its theological framework and hierarchical structure, Catholicism became the dominant

form of Christianity in Western Europe and beyond. However, Arianism gained and maintained weighty influence and support among Germanic tribes, including the Visigoths and Ostrogoths, who adopted this belief as they converted from pagan religions to Christianity.

Returning to the political intrigue at hand, after Theodoric died in 526 CE, tensions between the Goths and Romans escalated. Byzantine Emperor Justinian I (r. 527–565 CE) seized the opportunity to reassert imperial control over Italy and launched a military campaign. Driven by a relentless ambition to restore the former glory of the Roman Empire, he dispatched his loyal general, Belisarius, in 535 CE to recapture Italy from the Ostrogoths.

However, the Gothic War (535–554 CE) was far from a swift and easy conquest. The Byzantines faced fierce resistance from the Ostrogothic forces, and the conflict spanned nearly two decades, with both sides engaged in a grueling and protracted struggle for dominance. Finally, in 553 CE, at the Battle of Mons Lactarius, the Byzantines, led by General Narses, defeated the last Ostrogothic king, Teïas, ending their rule in Italy and establishing Byzantine Italy.

The Ostrogothic Kingdom was crucial in transitioning from Roman rule to Germanic domination in Italy.

Theodoric's policies, aimed at blending Gothic and Roman elements, left a lasting impact on the subsequent history of the land. The kingdom's cultural patronage and preservation of Roman heritage influenced the development of arts, architecture, and intellectual pursuits. The Byzantine conquest that followed marked a new phase in Italy's history, shaping its political and cultural outlook in the centuries to come.

Italy, under Byzantine rule, had a well-defined political and administrative structure. As a province of the Byzantine Empire, Italy was governed by an appointed Exarch serving as the emperor's representative. The Exarchate of Ravenna, established in the 6th century CE, emerged as the political and administrative center of the region. The Exarch, residing in Ravenna, held authority over a considerable portion of the Italian peninsula, particularly the central and northeastern areas. Responsible for maintaining imperial control, defending Byzantine interests, and overseeing the province's administration, the Exarch of Ravenna wielded significant power, including military command, judicial matters, tax collection, and general governance. Byzantine administrative practices, including taxation systems, legal codes, and administrative divisions, left a mark on the regions under Byzantine rule. Some Italian cities, such as Venice, later adopted elements of Byzantine administrative structures in their governance.

However, despite the Byzantine Empire's Roman origins, the spread of their rule altered Italy's cultural output. During their years stationed in Constantinople, the Eastern Roman Empire had adopted various practices of art and architecture that significantly differentiated them from their Western brethren. Byzantine mosaics, characterized by intricate designs, vibrant colors, religious motifs, and their signature gold background, adorned churches and public buildings. The Basilica of San Vitale in Ravenna and the Basilica of Sant'Apollinare Nuovo are prime examples of Byzantine-influenced architecture in Italy. These structures featured domes, arches, and ornate decorations that reflected signature Byzantine aesthetics.

Furthermore, although Orthodox Christianity—the primary religion of the Byzantine Empire—did not formally split from the Catholic Church until the Great Schism of 1054 CE, some uniquely Byzantine religious traditions still crept over to Italy at this time. One such practice would be the use and veneration of religious icons, though the use of icons in worship would become a source of great controversy later in the Byzantine Empire.

Another significant change during Byzantine rule was the influx of the Byzantine Greek language. Latin had reigned supreme during the time of the Romans, and Ostrogothic was introduced by the Germanic tribes. However, Byzantine Greek was the primary language for writing and administration. Luckily, Byzantine scholars and texts played a role in preserving and transmitting Greek and Roman knowledge to the Italian Renaissance. Without them, much of the ancient wisdom from Greece and Rome might have been lost to the ages. The literary and intellectual endeavors of later Italian writers and thinkers like Dante Alighieri were influenced by such works.

Yet, despite all this art, power, influence, and growth, the Byzantine Empire faced mounting pressures at home and abroad that seriously impaired its ability to maintain long-term control over the Italian peninsula. The first of such challenges was the rising strength of yet another Germanic tribe.

The Lombards, originating from northern Europe, began their migration southward in the late 6th century CE. In 568 CE, they invaded Italy, seeking to establish their own independent kingdom, and swiftly conquered large portions of the peninsula, including northern and central regions. They established their capital at Pavia and founded the Lombard Kingdom, or alternately, the Kingdom of the Lombards.

With a foothold in Italy, the Lombards continued their assault on the Byzantine territories under a series of aggressive and capable kings. For several decades, as the Byzantines struggled to control Italy, the Lombards continued adding more land to their domain, pushing the Byzantines out to the fringes of the Italian coast. Eventually, the Lombard Kingdom covered a substantial portion of Italy, with the Byzantine Empire retaining control over the Exarchate of Ravenna and some coastal cities, notably Venice.

The Lombard incursion brought noteworthy changes to Italy's political and cultural makeup. Establishing a distinct Germanic kingdom, characterized by their own legal code (the Lombard laws), customs, and political institutions, their rule introduced a decentralized system of governance, with power held by Lombard dukes ruling over various duchies within the kingdom. This kind of decentralized governance continued to be the norm throughout Italy until its eventual reunification in 1861 CE.

Yet, their presence was not a case of all-out dominance. The Lombards also interacted and assimilated with the existing Roman population, adopting aspects of Roman culture and administration. This led to a fusion of

Germanic and Roman influences within their kingdom. Italy was now semi-fragmented, divided between various Lombard duchies, Byzantine-controlled territories, and independent city-states. The Duchy of Benevento in southern Italy was one of these independent regions. Though ruled by Lombard dukes, it was the most unconstrained of all the duchies since the steadily growing papal territories around Rome separated it from the Lombard Kingdom's central portion.

The Lombard Kingdom survived for over two centuries, but in 774 CE, a Frankish king came calling, one with his sights set on far greater ambitions than just Italy: Charlemagne. He was the ruler of the Franks, a Germanic people who inhabited the region corresponding to present-day France, Belgium, the Netherlands, and parts of Germany during the early medieval years. They emerged as a prominent group during the Migration Period (500–1500 CE), and their rising presence just prior to that is thought to have contributed to the eventual fall of the Western Roman Empire.

Also known as Charles the Great, Charlemagne ruled from 768 to 814 CE and expanded his regional Frankish kingdom into a vast empire known as the Carolingian Empire. As one of the most memorable and powerful rulers in medieval Europe,

Charlemagne's reign marked the peak of Frankish power and the beginning of the Carolingian Renaissance, characterized by a cultural and intellectual revival in the empire. The Franks' military prowess, political organization, and close alliance with the Church were central to their success and the establishment of Charlemagne's empire.

As stated previously, in the 8th century, Italy was divided into various Lombard duchies and the Papal States, with the Lombards being the dominant power. The Papacy sought assistance from external forces to protect itself against Lombard aggression. Pope Adrian I appealed to Charlemagne for assistance against the Lombards, and in 773 CE Charlemagne answered his call by crossing the Alps with his Frankish forces and launching a military campaign to protect the Pontiff's interests.

Systematically, the Frankish forces vanquished Lombardian strongholds, one after another. By 774 CE, Charlemagne had seized Pavia, the Lombard capital, and deposed King Desiderius (r. 757–774 CE), ending Lombard rule in Italy. In recognition of his military success, Charlemagne was crowned the King of the Lombards by Pope Adrian I. This further legitimized his authority over the conquered Lombard territories.

Charlemagne aimed to establish a united Christian empire in Europe, and the conquest of Italy was a step towards that goal. He sought to consolidate his power by implementing administrative and political reforms and spreading Christianity. Thus, Charlemagne's alliance with the Papacy continued, and he became a patron of the Church. The pope recognized Charlemagne's authority and supported his efforts. This close relationship between the Frankish rulers and the Papacy would have long-lasting implications for the future of Europe.

The Frankish invasion brought significant changes to Italy. Charlemagne's rule marked a shift from Lombard dominance to Frankish control. Unlike former conquerors Odoacer and Theodoric, Charlemagne was not interested in maintaining the administrative structure of his newly conquered lands. The Lombard aristocracy was largely replaced by Frankish nobles, who formed a ruling class in the region. He also initiated political reforms that introduced elements of Frankish governance to Italy. However, despite the upheaval, Italy experienced a period of relative peace and prosperity under Charlemagne's rule. He encouraged trade and supported the development of towns and cities. Charlemagne also tried to revive education and culture, establishing schools and promoting learning throughout his empire.

His reign and achievements had a profound impact on the subsequent history of Europe. Charlemagne's coronation as Holy Roman Emperor by Pope Leo III on Christmas Day 800 CE symbolized the revival of the Roman Empire and the renewal of the title "Emperor of the Romans" since the fall of the Western Roman Empire in 476 CE. It marked a dedication to carry on the memory of Rome in their governance that persists to this day.

After Charlemagne died in 814 CE, his empire was divided among his sons, and Italy became a part of the larger Carolingian realm. Over time, the Carolingian Empire weakened, and Italy saw the rise of local powers and the emergence of independent city-states.

The region continued to have local power struggles while the Byzantine Empire maintained its presence in southern Italy and Sicily. However, the Byzantine hold on Italy steadily weakened as the years passed. The empire faced constant pressure, first from the Lombards and then from the Franks, who sought to expand their territories and diminish Byzantine influence in Italy. Already debilitated by the establishment of the Lombard Kingdom, Byzantine power faded even further when Charlemagne entered the picture. The continuous fighting became a financial strain on the empire.

Constant military expenses and the cost of maintaining imperial administration stretched resources thin. The local population often perceived Byzantine taxation policies as oppressive, contributing to dissatisfaction and resistance. Furthermore, internal imperial power struggles and conflicts diverted attention and resources away from Italy. Rival factions and court intrigue deteriorated the government and left Italy vulnerable to external pressures. By the 800s CE, the political instability within the empire truly hindered an effective response to the challenges in Italy. This trend would continue well into the next two centuries.

While the Byzantines attempted to manage the unchecked expansion of the new Frankish king to the north, a new problem entered from the south: a group of Arabic people, sometimes referred to as Moors or Saracens. Initial Muslim incursions into Sicily began towards the end of the 8th century CE. These mainly were Arab and Berber Muslims who came to the island as raiders and gradually established control.

In 827 CE, a prominent Arab expedition was launched against Sicily under the leadership of Asad ibn al-Furat. The Byzantines suffered a series of defeats, and by 831 CE, the Muslims had captured Palermo, the Byzantine capital of Sicily. Later that same year, the Emirate of Sicily was formally established by Emir Ziyadat Allah I of the Aghlabid dynasty, the rulers of Ifriqiya (present-day Tunisia and eastern Algeria).

The Aghlabids controlled Ifriqiya on behalf of the larger Abbasid Caliphate that ruled most of the Middle East and a large portion of North Africa. Under Muslim rule, Sicily grew into a prosperous and cosmopolitan center. The emirate's capital was Palermo, which became a thriving city known for its architectural achievements, vibrant markets, and cultural diversity. Other major cities on the island included Syracuse and Catania.

The Muslim Emirate of Sicily held strong until 1091 CE, despite continual challenges from the Byzantines. In the end, a different people expelled the Muslim powers from the island: the Normans. A medieval people with Norse roots who emerged as a distinct group in the 10th century CE, the Normans established their homeland in an area in modern-day France known as Normandy. Renowned for their military prowess, ambitious conquests, and cultural achievements, they began expanding their territories beyond Normandy. One of the notable early achievements was the Norman conquest of England in 1066 CE. Led by William the Conqueror (also known as William I of England), the Normans defeated the English forces at the Battle of Hastings, leading to the Norman establishment of the Kingdom of England.

Aside from England, the Normans embarked on ambitious European and Mediterranean conquests. These expeditions included the Norman invasion of southern Italy, led by Robert Guiscard and his brother Roger. Gradually gaining ground in Sicily over thirty years, the Normans had conquered the island by the late 11th century CE and ended Muslim rule. The Norman Kingdom of Sicily was established, marking a momentous shift in the region's political landscape.

The Norman Kingdom of Sicily was particularly notable for its multicultural character. The Normans assimilated with the local Arab, Byzantine, and Lombard populations, creating a unique blend of cultures and fostering intellectual and cultural advancements. The Norman rulers of Sicily, such as Roger II and Frederick II, patronized the arts, sciences, and literature, creating a vibrant and cosmopolitan court. With its strategic location, diverse cultural influences, and flourishing trade economy, the Kingdom of Sicily became a major center of power and innovation during the medieval era.

Returning to the mainland of Italy after the death of Charlemagne in 814 CE, the Carolingian Empire, which encompassed a large portion of Western Europe, began to face challenges. It was an empire built around one man's strength and charisma rather than the nation's power. When the empire was divided among Charlemagne's sons, this fragmentation profoundly affected Italy and its political future.

Without Charlemagne's strong personality holding the empire together, Italy experienced a period of political instability as various local powers emerged and sought to assert their authority. Charlemagne's sons and the following Carolingian kings struggled to maintain control over Italy. Still, in the end, the local nobles and bishops often wielded consequential power in their respective regions.

One of the key developments during this time was the rise of independent city-states. The cities in Italy, such as Venice, Milan, Florence, and Genoa, began to assert their autonomy and develop their governments and economies. These city-states became important centers of commerce, culture, and political power, shaping the future of Italy.

There was also a remarkable rise in papal power. The Papal or Pontifical States had begun to grow as early as the 8th century CE. However, it was under the reign of Pope Stephen II (r. 752–757 CE) and his successors that the land holdings of the Papacy expanded further. The most significant donation came from Pepin the Short (or Pippin), King of the Franks and Charlemagne's father. After warring with the Lombards, he gifted some territories he had won to the pope in 756 CE. Known as the Donation of Pepin (Pippin), this donation included the Exarchate of Ravenna and some other territories in central Italy.

Charlemagne further enlarged the Papal States during the late 8th and early 9th centuries CE. He confirmed and expanded the previous donations, granting additional territories and privileges to the Papacy. Though the lands held by the Roman Pontiff have dwindled over the ensuing centuries, the Vatican City within Rome remains an independent city-state, serving as the spiritual and administrative headquarters of the Catholic Church.

Aside from the land mass the papacy was steadily acquiring, the pope also began to play a crucial role in the political affairs of Italy, with popes seeking alliances and protection from external powers, often turning to the Carolingian rulers and later to the emperors of the Holy Roman Empire. This interaction between the Papacy and secular monarchs would become a defining characteristic of Italian politics in the following centuries.

Aside from seeking agreements with secular leaders, the Catholic Church also used its ability to create doctrines and religious laws to its advantage. A series of reforms enacted by Pope Gregory VII (r. 1073–1085 CE) aimed to address various issues within the Church, particularly focusing on the papacy's independence and power. Known as the Gregorian Reforms, these measures sought to strengthen the capacity and autonomy of the papacy by asserting its authority over secular rulers, curbing simony (the buying and selling of ecclesiastical offices), and combating clerical marriage and lay investiture.

Pope Gregory VII worked to assert papal supremacy through these reforms, meaning that the pope held ultimate authority over the Church, including secular rulers and bishops. He thoroughly believed it was his duty as the Vicar of Christ on Earth to depose secular rulers if deemed unfit or acting against the Church's best interests.

Gregory VII also strove to eliminate what he saw as moral quandaries bedeviling the Church. Chief among his complaints was the widespread practice of simony. This was rampant during the medieval period, with ecclesiastical offices bought and sold for financial gain. To stamp it out, Gregory VII decreed that the buying or selling of Church offices was invalid and threatened any individual involved with the punishment of excommunication.

Another thorn in Gregory VII's side was clerical matrimony. He heavily promoted celibacy for the priesthood, believing that married clergy were far more susceptible to secular influences and conflicts of interest than those who remained single and chaste. Lastly, he did away with the practice of lay investiture. Until the Gregorian Reforms, it was common for secular rulers to appoint bishops and other church officials that resided within their various kingdoms. Gregory VII considered this an infringement on the Church's independence and authority. He argued that only the pope, the spiritual head of the Church, had the right to appoint bishops.

The reforms initiated by Gregory VII met intense resistance from secular rulers, particularly Emperor Henry IV (r. 1084–1105 CE) of the Holy Roman Empire. The Investiture Controversy, a conflict between the pope and the emperor over the appointment of bishops, became a foremost issue during this period and lasted for several decades.

Ultimately, the Gregorian Reforms had a profound and lasting impact on the structure and authority of the Catholic Church and thus had a lasting effect on the course of history in Italy. They laid the groundwork for the strengthening of papal power, the development of canon law, and the assertion of the Church's independence from secular authorities. The reforms also set the stage for future conflicts and power struggles between the papacy and secular rulers, laying the groundwork for the events in medieval Europe.

Beyond the expansions of the papacy in the center of the peninsula, Italy faced invasions and raids from all angles. Arab raiders from North Africa attacked coastal regions, while the Magyars, a nomadic people from the east, raided and skirmished along the northern borders. Additionally, local princes and nobles were locked into petty power squabbles, leading to further fragmentation and disorganization.

Amid all this chaos, the Byzantine presence in Italy was on its last legs. The empire's influence and control over trade and diplomacy waned as regional powers coalesced into prominent city-states like Venice and Genoa. By the 11th century CE, the threat of the Seljuk Turks to the east of Byzantine Anatolia (a portion of present-day Türkiye) diverted attention and resources away from their holdings on the Italian peninsula. The Normans shattered the last vestiges of Byzantine control in Italy when they swept into the southern portion during their campaign that began in Sicily.

The Byzantines' last stand occurred in the coastal town of Bari, a strategic port town on the Adriatic Sea. The siege of Bari, which took place from 1068 to 1071 CE, was a major military conflict between the Normans and the Byzantine Empire. Bari had been under Byzantine control for many years, but the Normans, led by Robert Guiscard, laid siege to the city in an effort to expand their territorial holdings. The siege lasted three years, but ultimately, the Normans wore down the Byzantine defenses and emerged victorious. The conquest of Bari marked a key milestone in the Norman expansion in southern Italy, solidifying their control over the region.

The loss of Italy was a blow to the Byzantine Empire, and it would continue to shrink in the following centuries. It was eliminated as a political entity in 1453 CE when Constantinople, its capital, fell to the Ottoman Turks, marking the end of the long and illustrious history of the Byzantine civilization.

The politics within Italy continued to evolve throughout the medieval period, with the emergence of powerful city-states, the influence of the papacy, and the involvement of foreign powers. The struggle for power and the complexities of regional politics laid the foundation for the Italian Renaissance and paved the way for the Golden Age of the Italian city-states.

As the curtain falls on this chapter of Italian history, the echoes of the Byzantine Empire, the struggles between Lombards and Franks, and the rise and fall of powerful city-states all intertwine to form a colorful array of narratives. After the failure of the Byzantines on the peninsula, Italy would not be reunified for centuries yet to come, and bitter power struggles between wealthy and influential factions were on the horizon. Yet, despite the chaos and uncertainty, seeds of artistic brilliance were sown, laying the foundation for a cultural rebirth that awaited its grand debut.

4

ITALY'S RADIANT REBIRTH: THE TRANSITION FROM THE MIDDLE AGES TO THE RENAISSANCE (1100–1600 CE)

T he transition from the 12th century to the dawning of the Italian Renaissance in the 14th century witnessed a profound evolution across the Italian peninsula. As the feudal order of the Middle Ages gradually gave way to a more urban and mercantile society, Italian city-states flourished as vibrant centers of commerce, culture, and intellectual exchange. Trade routes connected Italy to the affluent markets of the East, fueling economic prosperity and fostering a spirit of innovation. Amidst this backdrop, the seeds of artistic and intellectual revival were sown as ancient texts from Greece and Rome resurfaced, inspiring a new generation of thinkers. The stage was set for a remarkable period of rebirth, where pursuing knowledge, celebrating human potential, and the transformative power of artistic expression would ignite the flame of the Italian Renaissance.

However, before the Renaissance burst forth in full force, some developments in Italy reshaped the peninsula's political lines. To the south, the Normans had ruled in Sicily since they expelled the Saracens roughly a century before. However, when King William II of Sicily (r. 1166–1189 CE) died, there was a bit of a succession crisis. His aunt, Princess Constance, laid claim to the Sicilian throne following his death. Unfortunately for her, the Sicilians favored her illegitimate nephew, Tancred of Lecce (r. 1189–1194), and a war between the two sides ensued. The princess happened to be married to Henry VI (r. 1191–1197) of the Hohenstaufen dynasty, and when the pair were crowned Holy Roman Emperor and Empress in Rome in 1191 CE, her elevation in status certainly aided her cause.

However, when Tancred died three years later, Henry VI and Constance were able to assume the throne of Sicily with minimal bloodshed. Tancred's young son William III (r. 1194) was deposed and sent to Hohenems in present-day Austria, where he later died, likely murdered at the hands of Hohenstaufen deputies. His deposition brought a decisive end to Norman rule on the island. The Hohenstaufens did not hold the kingdom for long, though, and throughout the ensuing century, Sicily changed hands more than once.

By 1282 CE, the island had passed to the Capetian House of Anjou—a cadet branch of the French royal House of Capet. During Easter that year, there was a violent uprising known as the Sicilian Vespers. During a celebration of Vespers (evening prayer in the Catholic tradition) in the church of Santo Spirito in Palermo, a clash broke out between the local population and French soldiers. This incident escalated into a wide-spread revolt, with Sicilians attacking and killing French residents and soldiers throughout the city. The rebellion quickly spread across the island as the Sicilian population rose up against the Angevin rulers, ousting Charles I of Anjou (r. 1266–1285 CE) from his throne.

Thus, the Sicilian throne was passed to Peter III of Aragon (Peter I of Sicily) (r. 1282–1285 CE) through his wife Constance II's claim. She was the daughter of the last Hohenstaufen king of Sicily before the French took the island. However, the Angevins did not relinquish their claim to Sicily so easily. They retained control over the southern mainland territories of the Kingdom, which included the city of Naples. Over time, these territories evolved into a separate entity known as the Kingdom of Naples. However, it was still formally called the Kingdom of Sicily for a time, with the island kingdom often referred to as "Sicily beyond the Lighthouse" or Trinacria.

As the lines on the map shifted in the south, a bitter dispute bubbled up to the north. The conflict between the Guelphs (or Guelf) and the Ghibellines was one of the more prominent political and social rivalries that gripped various regions of Italy during the late Middle Ages, particularly from the 12th to the 14th century CE. Originating from a dispute over the imperial and papal powers, the conflict became deeply intertwined with regional politics, power struggles, and allegiances.

The Guelphs and the Ghibellines took their names from prominent political factions of the time. The Guelphs derived their name from the Welf family (in Italian, "Guelfo"), who supported the pope's authority and advocated for the supremacy of the Papal States over the imperial rule of the Holy Roman Emperors. The Ghibellines, on the other hand, drew their name from the Hohenstaufen family, known as the "Waiblingen" in German (in Italian, "Ghibellino"), who championed the authority of the Holy Roman Emperor.

The conflict between these factions manifested differently across Italian city-states, with alliances and rivalries varying from one region to another. Cities like Florence, Bologna, and Perugia became focal points of Guelph influence, while Ghibelline sympathies often prevailed in cities like Pisa, Siena, and Arezzo. The conflict was not limited to political ideologies but also encompassed economic, social, and cultural divisions, with each faction attracting different classes and social groups. Typically, the Guelphs were a relatively newly wealthy group from the mercantile class, while the Ghibellines tended to be landed nobles whose families had long been feudal lords.

The Guelph-Ghibelline conflict resulted in prolonged power struggles, feuds, and armed clashes between rival factions. It led to political instability and intermittent warfare throughout Italy, with shifting allegiances and the intervention of external powers, such as the Papacy and the Holy Roman Empire, further complicating the situation. The conflict peaked during the 13th century CE, culminating in violent clashes and the rise of powerful city-states like Florence and Milan.

Over time, the Guelph-Ghibelline conflict gradually lost its original ideological significance and trans-formed into a broader struggle for power and control between rival factions within Italian city-states. By the 14th century CE, the conflict began to wane, giving way to other political and social dynamics.

Although the Guelphs and the Ghibellines eventually faded as distinct political entities, their legacy and the memories of their conflicts left a lasting impact on

Italian history and culture. The rivalries and divisions between factions became intertwined with regional identities, shaping political alliances and cultural traditions that persisted long after the conflict subsided. The prominent poet Dante Alighieri became embroiled in the Guelph-Ghibelline conflict, supporting the Guelph faction, and was exiled from Florence as a result. Even though Florence was a Guelph stronghold, there was infighting within the Guelph supporters. Dante aligned himself with the White Guelphs, a faction within the Guelph party that opposed papal influence and sought greater independence for Florence. In 1301 CE, the Black Guelphs, a rival faction, gained the upper hand in Florence's political scene and accused Dante and other White Guelphs of financial irregularities and corruption.

As a result, Dante was banished from Florence and faced exile. He was sentenced to pay a hefty fine and, if unpaid, to be burned at the stake. Dante, unwilling to submit to these terms, chose to remain in exile and never returned to his beloved city. The experience inspired him to pen his enduring masterpiece, *The Divine Comedy (La divina commedia),* which shaped Italian literature and language while offering a profound commentary on the struggles of his time.

Often referred to as the "Father of the Italian Language," he is primarily remembered for his significant contributions to the development and standardization of Italian. In his renowned epic poem, he broke away from the prevailing tradition of writing in Latin. Instead, he composed his work in the vernacular Tuscan dialect, which later became the basis for modern Italian. Immortalized in part thanks to Dante's work, the Guelph-Ghibelline conflict is a testament to the complex dynamics of power, ideology, and regionalism in medieval Italy.

With the 1200s ending, the stage was set for a significant shift in Italian life. In the chronicles of European history, there exists a period that shines as a resplendent dawn, illuminating the path of civilization with extraordinary brilliance. This era, known as the Renaissance, unfolded first across the captivating landscape of Italy, and its echoes reverberated throughout Europe. Emerging from the fertile soil of Italian communes and city-states, the Renaissance bloomed as a testament to the indomitable spirit of curiosity, creativity, and intellectual fervor. It was a time when the assumptions of the medieval past were shattered, giving birth to an era that celebrated the triumph of human potential, transforming the realms of art, literature, science, and governance. From this period, the Italy of magnificent palaces, soaring cathedrals, and enlightened minds arose, forever changing how the world would view the region's legacy.

Though the dates vary depending on the source, most agree it spanned roughly from the 14th to the 16th centuries CE. This era emerged as a vibrant rebirth of classical ideals and artistic expression within Italy, particularly in Florence, Milan, and Venice. The Renaissance was a remarkable surge in human creativity, scientific inquiry, and philosophical exploration.

At its core, it was a reaction against the prevailing medieval mindset. Inspired by the rediscovery of ancient Greek and Roman texts, scholars and thinkers sought to revive the spirit of classical antiquity. The result was humanism, a philosophical movement emphasizing the worth and potential of human beings, and it became a driving force behind the Renaissance. It celebrated the virtues of reason, individualism, and the pursuit of knowledge across various disciplines.

Art also played an exceptional role in the Renaissance, as artists sought to capture the beauty of the natural world and the essence of humanity. Masters like Leonardo da Vinci, Michelangelo, and Raphael infused their works with a new level of realism and emotional depth, employing techniques such as chiaroscuro (the use of contrast between light and dark) and linear perspective to create lifelike paintings and sculptures.

This period witnessed the birth of iconic masterpieces like da Vinci's *Mona Lisa* and Michelangelo's *David*, which continue to enrapture audiences today.

However, as mentioned above, the Renaissance was not solely confined to art but also extended to science, literature, and philosophy. Scholars such as Galileo Galilei and Nicolaus Copernicus challenged prevailing beliefs about the nature of the universe, paving the way for a scientific revolution. Intellectual giants like Dante and Francesco Petrarch revitalized literature, penning influential works that explored human emotions, societal issues, and the human condition. Moreover, the spread of the printing press in the 15th century CE facilitated the dissemination of knowledge and ideas, leading to exponential growth in intellectual pursuits.

With its zeal for humanism, artistic excellence, and intellectual exploration, the Italian Renaissance altered the course of history. It became a bridge connecting the classical past to the modern world, influencing subsequent movements such as the Enlightenment and shaping the trajectory of Western civilization. The shadows of the Renaissance's cultural, artistic, and intellectual achievements continue to inspire creatives and scientists today.

So what was the fertile political ground that ensured such an explosion of creative and cerebral endeavors was possible? With the departure of the Byzantine powers, the expulsion of the Saracens, and the fracturing of various Lombard and Frankish kingdoms, Italy, as a unified idea, ceased to exist. Instead, Italy had a collection of independent city-states, also known as communes. Various factors influenced the rise of communes. The economic prosperity of Italian cities, fueled by trade and commerce, allowed the growth of a wealthy merchant class. As these merchants amassed wealth and influence, they sought greater political control over their cities.

In contrast to much of Europe at the time, these communes were not usually governed—on paper at least—by a king or a single ruler. Instead, though the political structure of communes varied, they generally operated as republics. Power was typically concentrated in the hands of a group of wealthy families known as the *popolo grasso* (fat people). However, some communes experimented with democratic elements, with broader participation from the *popolo minuto* (small people), comprising artisans, laborers, and other lower classes.

A commune's government might look something like this: elected officials administered the city and made decisions on behalf of the commune. Then, these officials were organized into councils or assemblies, which deliberated on matters of governance, legislation, and defense. These communes emerged as centers of economic and political power and were often controlled mainly by a few wealthy merchant families. Three of the largest—Florence, Milan, and Venice—will be briefly discussed.

Nestled amidst the lush landscapes of Tuscany, Florence emerged as a beacon of artistic brilliance and intellectual enlightenment. Originally founded as a Roman settlement, it blossomed during the medieval period into a flourishing commune. The rise of wealthy merchant families—the most prominent being the famous and scheming Medici—fueled the city's economic prosperity, and their patronage transformed Florence into a thriving hub of commerce and culture. In the heart of Florence, the magnificent Duomo, with its majestic dome designed by Filippo Brunelleschi, stood as a testament to the city's architectural prowess. The project, which the Medici family funded, took seventy-two years to construct, from 1296 to 1368 CE.

It was not only in the realm of architecture that Florence flourished. The city became a cradle of artistic innovation, nurturing the talents of visionaries like Leonardo da Vinci, Michelangelo, and Botticelli, who left an indelible mark on art history. As a center of humanist thought, Florence fostered intellectual luminaries like Niccolò Machiavelli, whose groundbreaking works, most notably *The Prince,* challenged conventional political wisdom.

Deep in the heart of Lombardy, Milan rose from its humble origins to become a powerhouse of industry, political intrigue, and Renaissance splendor. Overcoming periods of foreign domination, the city evolved into a leading center of commerce and craftsmanship. Its strategic location along crucial trade routes propelled Milan's economic growth, attracting skilled artisans and craftsmen from all corners of Europe.

Milan attained political prominence under the reign of the ambitious Visconti and Sforza families, transforming the city into a vibrant courtly center. It was here that, despite his Florentine origins, the genius of Leonardo da Vinci flourished, his artistic and scientific pursuits nurtured by the patronage of the ruling elites. Milan's architectural achievements, exemplified by the magnificent Sforza Castle and the breathtaking Duomo di Milano, still stand as majestic testaments to the city's Renaissance grandeur. From the realms of fashion and design to the realms of military might and intellectual curiosity, Milan's multifaceted legacy continues to resonate as a testament to its enduring significance.

Venice, the enchanting "Queen of the Adriatic," emerged as a dominant maritime republic, captivating the world with its unparalleled beauty, opulence, and political astuteness. Built upon a lagoon, the city's unique geography bestowed it with a strategic advantage in Mediterranean trade, allowing Venice to flourish as a thriving commercial hub. Its merchant ships traversed vast seas, establishing trade networks that extended to Constantinople, the Middle East, and beyond.

The Republic of Venice was governed by a complex system of elected officials and overseen by the Doge, the chief magistrate and the elected leader of the city-state. Venice upheld a tradition of political stability, creating an environment conducive to cultural and artistic innovation. The city's iconic architectural gems, such as the mesmerizing St. Mark's Basilica and the graceful Rialto Bridge, exemplified the fusion of Byzantine, Gothic, and Renaissance influences that defined Venetian aesthetics. Venice became a haven for artistic luminaries, including Titian, Tintoretto, and Giovanni Bellini, whose masterpieces adorned palaces and churches, immortalizing the city's cultural opulence. Venice's reputation as a cradle of maritime supremacy and refined artistic expression continues to capture the imagination of millions.

These three city-states and other notable ones, like Genoa, Naples, and Siena, fiercely guarded their autonomy and often engaged in conflicts with neighboring communes to gain and maintain prosperity. The struggle for power and resources led to rivalries, alliances, and occasional warfare between city-states. Prominent examples include the conflicts between Florence and Siena or the long-standing rivalry between Genoa and Venice.

With so many conflicting powers, Italy experienced a turbulent and fragmented political landscape marked by numerous conflicts, wars, and skirmishes. The city-states, with their independent governments and rivalries, were often at the center of these disputes, driven by power struggles, territorial ambitions, and competing interests.

One significant conflict during this period was the Italian Wars (1494–1559), which involved major European powers and Italian city-states. The wars were characterized by shifting alliances and the intervention of foreign forces seeking to exert their influence over Italian territories. Under King Charles VIII (r. 1483–1498 CE) and later King Francis I (r. 1515–1547 CE), the French made several incursions into Italy, igniting conflicts involving city-states like Florence, Milan, and Venice. The wars resulted in significant political upheaval and devastation, with battles fought on Italian soil and the interference of foreign powers leaving lasting scars on the region.

In addition to external conflicts, internal power struggles among Italian city-states played a significant role. One in Florence, the Pazzi Conspiracy, will be discussed. Similar power struggles occurred in other city-states like Milan, where rival factions vied for control, leading to shifting alliances and armed confrontations.

The Pazzi Conspiracy, an infamous event that unfolded in Florence in 1478 CE, is a significant chapter in the history of Renaissance Italy. Orchestrated by the Pazzi family, in collaboration with Pope Sixtus IV (r. 1471–1484 CE) and his nephew Girolamo Riario, the conspiracy aimed to topple the ruling Medici family and seize control of Florence, setting the stage for a gripping tale of power, betrayal, and political upheaval.

The Pazzi family, influential bankers and rivals of the Medici dynasty, harbored longstanding resentment towards their dominant counterparts in Florence. Eager to reclaim their erstwhile prominence, they plotted to remove the Medici from their position of authority, built on a foundation of wealth, political savvy, and patronage of the arts.

Under the cloak of secrecy, the Pazzi family allied with Pope Sixtus IV and his nephew, Girolamo Riario, aiming to orchestrate a decisive blow against the Medici brothers, Lorenzo and Giuliano. The conspirators planned to strike during a solemn religious service held within the hallowed walls of the Florence Cathedral under the Duomo that Lorenzo and Giuliano's grandfather, Cosimo, had financed.

On the fateful day of April 26, 1478 CE, as Easter Sunday Mass commenced, the unsuspecting Medici brothers found themselves amid a grand conspiracy. Francesco de' Pazzi and an accomplice named Bernardo Baroncelli ruthlessly attacked Giuliano de' Medici, fatally striking him down. However, fortune smiled upon Lorenzo de' Medici, who narrowly escaped the clutches of death, albeit bearing the scars of the treacherous assault.

Despite the audacious assassination attempt, the Pazzi conspirators' grand design to incite a popular uprising against the Medici rule failed to materialize. Instead, the citizens of Florence rallied around the Medici, fiercely defending their established order. The Pazzi were swiftly condemned, their ill-fated cause deserted by the very populace they had sought to incite.

The repercussions of the Pazzi Conspiracy were grave. Many of the conspirators, including Francesco de'

Pazzi and his uncle, Jacopo de' Pazzi, faced the grim fate of execution. Meanwhile, Lorenzo de' Medici, with the unwavering support of the Florentine populace, consolidated his family's authority and ensured the continuation of their influential reign.

The failed plot also shaped the trajectory of Florence. The Medici family, emboldened by their triumph over adversity, solidified their dominance, guiding the city's destiny for generations to come. Moreover, this failed assassination attempt catalyzed the ensuing flowering of the Renaissance in Florence under the patronage and stewardship of Lorenzo de' Medici, later known as Lorenzo the Magnificent.

The Papal States, centered in Rome, were not immune to conflicts. The Italian city-states often found themselves entangled in disputes with the papacy as popes sought to extend their influence and control over neighboring territories. Pope Julius II (r. 1503–1513 CE), known for his military prowess, engaged in military campaigns to expand the Papal States, which included clashes with rival city-states and foreign powers.

Furthermore, the conflicts of the Renaissance were not solely militaristic. Artistic rivalries, intellectual debates, and political intrigues also shaped the cultural and social landscape of the time. For instance, the rivalry between Leonardo da Vinci and Michelangelo, two of the era's greatest artistic geniuses, was not limited to their creative pursuits but also involved personal and professional rivalries, leading to intense competition and clashes of egos.

Aside from military might, patronage of the arts and culture proved to be another way communes flexed their influence. Wealthy merchant families supported the arts by commissioning works from renowned artists and scholars. This patronage contributed to the advancements in literature, painting, sculpture, and architecture that defined the development of the Italian Renaissance.

The disputes in Renaissance Italy were multi-faceted and interconnected, involving military confrontations, political power struggles, and artistic spats. These conflicts left a lasting impact on the region, shaping its political boundaries, cultural development, and historical memory. The turbulent nature of the era, with its constant state of flux and competition, contributed to the remarkable artistic, intellectual, and political achievements that defined the Renaissance period.

As discussed, a vast amount of new wealth allowed for military campaigns and fantastic artistic and literary endeavors that characterized the Italian city-states of the Renaissance. Italian city-states, such as Venice,

Genoa, and Florence, cultivated strategic relationships along main trade routes, including the Mediterranean and the Silk Road. Amassing wealth and power through maritime trade, these city-states often acted as intermediaries between Europe, Asia, and Africa. They developed extensive trading networks, establishing colonies and trading posts in Constantinople, Alexandria, and the Levant.

Prominent Italian explorers like Marco Polo embarked on ambitious journeys to the East, documenting their travels and encounters with different cultures. Marco Polo's book, *The Travels of Marco Polo*, was widely read and sparked curiosity about distant lands and new trade opportunities.

Italian merchants were pioneers in the exploration and establishment of trading routes. They ventured into the Atlantic Ocean, charting new paths and reaching as far as West Africa, the Canary Islands, and the Americas. Notably, Christopher Columbus, an Italian explorer sponsored by the Spanish Crown, landed in the so-called "New World" in 1492 CE, opening up a new era of transatlantic exploration and trade. However, it is important to note that this connection between the Americas and Europe did not have purely favorable consequences. Present-day history has accurately seen the exploits of Columbus and his counterparts and contemporaries for the destructive force they were on the native populations of Africa, the Americas, and the Caribbean.

Italian merchants and banking families, such as the Medici in Florence, were vital in financing and facilitating these trade ventures. They introduced innovative banking practices, such as bills of exchange and letters of credit, which enabled international commerce and the banking industry's growth.

The wealth accumulated from trade had a profound impact on Italian cities. Thanks to their newfound riches, wealthy merchants became patrons, commissioning renowned artists and architects to create magnificent works that still stand as testaments to this era, such as the previously noted works of Leonardo da Vinci, Michelangelo, and Brunelleschi.

Italian exploration and trade during this period expanded horizons, stimulated cultural exchange, and contributed to the economic and intellectual prosperity of the Italian city-states. The voyages of Italian explorers and the establishment of trade networks laid the groundwork for future global exploration and the interconnectivity of nations.

Although the independence of the city-states did not endure into the present day, their moment in the sun had a lasting impact on the country's political and social landscape. Setting the stage for the later formation of larger states, the city-state governance model also influenced other European regions and became an essential template for forming modern nation-states.

While secular institutions have mainly been discussed thus far, it is important to remember that religious institutions, particularly the Catholic Church, held just as much (and sometimes more) political power at this time. After the Concordat of Worms in 1122 CE solved the Investiture Controversy mentioned in the previous chapter by recognizing the authority of the Church in appointing bishops, the pope's power continued to grow. Beyond its evident domination in religious matters, the papacy and the Church also played a crucial role in cultural and intellectual life. The Church was a significant patron of the arts, supporting the development of magnificent cathedrals, sculptures, paintings, and illuminated manuscripts. Notable artists, such as Giotto di Bondone and Fra Angelico, were commissioned by the Church to create religious artworks.

The Catholic Church's influence extended beyond Rome, with various monastic orders and religious institutions spreading across Italy. These institutions served as centers of education, scholarship, and charitable activities. Monastic orders like the Benedictines, Franciscans, and Dominicans established schools and universities, fostering intellectual pursuits and contributing to learning and knowledge growth.

However, the Catholic Church also faced challenges during this period. The most dramatic was The Avignon Papacy, or the Babylonian Captivity. In brief, the papal court temporarily moved from Rome to Avignon, France, from 1309 to 1377 CE. This period marked a significant shift in the center of papal power and profoundly impacted the Catholic Church and its relationship with secular rulers.

The move of the papal court to Avignon was initiated by Pope Clement V (r. 1305–1314 CE), a Frenchman himself. Several factors contributed to this decision, including political pressures, conflicts within the Italian states, and the influence of the French monarchy under Philip IV (r. 1285–1314 CE). The popes who resided in Avignon during this period were often seen as under the French kings' influence and control.

The Avignon Papacy had both positive and negative consequences. On the positive side, it allowed for stability and centralized authority within the Catholic Church. The popes in Avignon initiated administrative and bureaucratic reforms, improved financial management, and focused on the organization of the Church.

However, relocating the papal court to Avignon led to criticism and controversy. The papacy became entangled in French politics and was seen as losing its independence and moral authority. The absence of the papacy from Rome raised questions about the legitimacy and spiritual significance of the popes based in Avignon.

The Avignon Papacy ended in 1377 CE with the election of Pope Gregory XI (r. 1370–1378 CE), who decided to return the papal court to Rome. However, the return to Rome did not completely resolve the issues within the Catholic Church, as it soon led to the Great Schism of 1378 CE. This split resulted in popes in Rome competing against rival "antipopes" in Avignon. This schism further weakened the authority and unity of the Church and was not resolved until 1417 CE with the Council of Constance.

Beyond the controversy of the Avignon Papacy, the later years of the Renaissance witnessed the beginnings of the Protestant Reformation, a movement that challenged certain practices and doctrines of the Catholic Church. The Reformation sparked theological debates and led to schisms within Christianity, significantly impacting the Catholic Church's influence and the religious landscape of Europe.

The Italian Renaissance was a period of remarkable achievements and transformative changes that left a lasting impact on art, culture, and society. The great intellectual and artistic growth, fueled by the patronage of wealthy merchants and influential families like the Medici, enabled the emergence of visionary figures whose names are still well-known today. However, the Renaissance was not without its challenges. It witnessed countless bouts of political instability, multiplying religious tensions, and continuous social inequalities.

Yet, amidst these difficulties, the Renaissance embodied the human spirit's boundless creativity, the pursuit of knowledge, and the desire to question established norms. Its legacy is a testament to the resilience and potential of human ingenuity, shaping the course of Western civilization for centuries to come. As the Renaissance came to a close, it paved the way for a new era of exploration, scientific advancements, and cultural shifts that would shape the course of history— the dawning of the Age of Enlightenment.

5

REACTION, REFORMATION, RESURGENCE: THE ENLIGHTENMENT (1500S – 1800 CE)

A s the Renaissance reached its apex, Italy experienced a shifting cultural and artistic landscape that marked the end of an epoch. The decline of the Renaissance came about due to changing political dynamics, evolving artistic tastes, economic challenges, and the impact of external forces. These shifts gave rise to the Baroque, a new artistic and cultural movement that swept across Italy and transformed the creative landscape, serving as a transitionary period that brought Italy closer to reunification and the modern era.

Plagued by political instability during the late 15th and early 16th centuries, Italy waded through various conflicts, wars, and power struggles among city-states and foreign occupiers. This naturally disrupted the thriving artistic and cultural environment of the Renaissance and diverted resources and attention away from the arts. One of the most pivotal events was the Sack of Rome in 1527 CE. Though the pope at the time was allied against Charles V, the Holy Roman Emperor (r. 1519–1556 CE), this attack by his Imperial Army, composed of Spanish and German troops, was not carried out under his orders. After defeating the French at Pavia two years earlier, the Imperial Army remained largely uncontested for power on the Italian peninsula. However, they had not been paid, and when the tired and hungry mercenaries mutinied, the poorly defended city of Rome did not stand a chance.

Under Pope Clement VII's rule (r. 1523–1534 CE), the city fell victim to brutal and devastating pillaging. The Imperial Army unleashed chaos, looting, and violence, destroying countless artworks, manuscripts, and historical treasures. The Sack of Rome symbolized a major turning point in the power dynamics of Italy, further destabilizing an already politically fragmented peninsula.

The consequences of the Sack of Rome reverberated throughout Italy and Europe. It shook the papacy's authority, highlighting the Church's vulnerability and the need for secular alliances and militaristic fortifications. The event also provoked outrage and condemnation, prompting a renewed sense of nationalism and identity among the Italian states as they sought to defend their territories against foreign invasions.

Moreover, the Sack of Rome is thought to have accelerated the decline of the Renaissance in Italy. Many artists, intellectuals, and scholars fled the city, dispersing their talents and ideas across Europe. The event also marked a transition towards a more turbulent and uncertain era, paving the way for the rise of the Baroque period, characterized by dramatic, emotional, and extravagant artistic expressions.

The sociopolitical turbulence directly impacted the economic well-being of the Italian city-states, which aided the decline of the High Renaissance. Economic crises, trade disruptions, and the shifting dynamics of the Italian economy impaired patrons' financial stability and limited their ability to support grand artistic projects.

Before the 1500s, the Mediterranean had enjoyed a seat of power in European trade. As a result, Italy had grown wealthy, particularly in port cities like Venice. However, discovering new sea routes during the Age of Exploration bolstered new maritime powers like Portugal and Spain. This diverted trade away from the Italian city-states, and the once-prosperous trade hubs saw a diminished economic influence. The Italian peninsula was also largely excluded from the morally reprehensible but lucrative Atlantic slave trade.

As a result, wealthy patrons could no longer fund artistic endeavors at the same rate they had previously enjoyed. Commissions declined, and financial support for artists evaporated, changing the momentum and output production of the Renaissance as a whole. Furthermore, artistic tastes and preferences began to evolve, with new styles and movements gaining popularity. The Baroque period, which followed the High Renaissance, introduced a more dynamic, dramatic, and emotionally charged approach to art. The allure of the Baroque style ultimately overshadowed the restrained and idealized qualities of the High Renaissance.

Beyond shifting cultural tastes, between the rise of the Protestant Reformation and the Catholic Church's reactionary Counter-Reformation, artistic creativity and freedoms were sharply curtailed in the name of religion. Censoring art and literature became common as the Catholic Church sought to maintain its supremacy over new Protestant factions. This grasp for power was fully illustrated by the Council of Trent, which declared not just humanism, but any view that challenged Catholic doctrine and authority as heresy.

Convened in 1545 CE, the Council of Trent was a landmark event in the history of the Catholic Church. This ecumenical council, held in the northern Italian city of Trent (Trento), aimed to address the religious challenges of the Protestant Reformation. Spanning over eighteen years, sessions ran intermittently from 1545 to 1563 CE. It brought together bishops, theologians, and church officials across Europe to discuss doctrine, discipline, and religious practices. The council sought to reaffirm Catholic teachings, clarify points of theological contention that had haunted the Church for years, and address perceived abuses within the Catholic leadership.

During its sessions, the Council of Trent issued decrees on various topics. It reaffirmed the authority of Church tradition alongside Scripture, emphasized the importance of the sacraments and liturgy, and upheld the doctrine of justification through faith and works. It addressed issues such as the interpretation of Scripture, the role of clergy, the veneration of saints and relics, and the education and training of priests.

Significant reforms within the Catholic Church were also initiated to combat some of the most egregious problems highlighted by Protestant detractors. Measures were taken to fight corruption and improve the moral conduct of the clergy, discouraging extravagant lifestyles among Church officials. The council also established seminaries for priests' proper education and training and standardized the liturgy by publishing the Roman Missal and Catechism. The decrees and reforms executed at the Council of Trent revitalized and solidified Catholic doctrine and practice, contributing to the Counter-Reformation and the reaffirmation of Catholic identity in the face of Protestant attacks. However, as noted above, the council's decisions stretched beyond religious life, influencing European art and culture and contributing to creative stifling within Renaissance artists.

Yet even without the pressure from religion, the classical realism of the Renaissance period was gradually being supplanted by two new styles: Mannerism and Baroque.

Mannerism was an artistic style that emerged in the late Renaissance, particularly in Italy. It can be seen as a reaction to and departure from the harmonious and balanced ideals of the High Renaissance. Seeking to break away from the classical perfection of their predecessors, Mannerist artists explored more individualistic, imaginative, and complex approaches to art. Notable characteristics of the Mannerist style include elongated limbs and distorted or contorted poses. This exaggeration aimed to create a sense of elegance, grace, and an otherworldly quality in the artwork.

Intricate and elaborate compositions were favored to add complexity, sophistication, and an air of intellectualism to the works, incorporating symbolism, allegory, and references to classical mythology. Appreciators of Mannerist art had to interpret and intellectually engage with the work before them. Additionally, color usage was often unconventional. Vibrant and exaggerated colors, intense contrast, and unnatural hues created a sense of heightened drama and emotional impact. Well-remembered Mannerist artists include Parmigianino, Jacopo Tintoretto, and El Greco.

While Mannerism was primarily an Italian phenomenon and was soon replaced, it also influenced European art and directly inspired aspects of Baroque art. Emerging in Europe during the 17th century CE, Baroque art is characterized by its dynamic and dramatic style and grandeur, emphasizing emotion, movement, and theatricality. One of the defining features of Baroque art is its use of dramatic lighting techniques, known as chiaroscuro. Artists built on the legacy of their Renaissance forefathers and skillfully employed light and shadow to create a sense of depth, three-dimensionality, and heightened drama. This technique allowed for the accentuation of focal points and created tension and contrast within the artwork.

Mainly, Baroque art is remembered for its opulence and ornamentation. Intricate details, elaborate decorations, and rich textures created visually captivating and luxurious compositions. Elaborate drapery, gilded surfaces, and complex architectural elements were typical, contributing to the overall splendor. Figures in Baroque art were often full of dynamic movement and energy, with exaggerated gestures and powerful expressions.

Religious themes were prevalent in Baroque art, as the Catholic Church heavily patronized many artists. Artworks often depicted scenes from biblical narratives, saints, and martyrs and aimed to elicit a deeply spiritual response from the viewer. Gian Lorenzo Bernini's sculpture *Ecstasy of St. Teresa* is an excellent example. Other prominent Baroque artists include Caravaggio, Peter Paul Rubens, and Artemisia Gentileschi. Their expressive and dynamic works set the stage for the later development of Rococo and Neoclassical art styles.

The vibrant artistic achievements of the Renaissance did more than set up the next few centuries of creative endeavors—they also paved the way for a remarkable intellectual transformation in Italy during the 16th and

17th centuries. The cerebral pursuits of the Renaissance directly shaped Italy's cultural landscape into a fertile ground for the seeds of the Scientific Revolution. The quest for understanding the natural world and unlocking its secrets became an endeavor that captivated the minds of scholars, scientists, and philosophers. The same spirit of curiosity and exploration that characterized the artistic innovations of the Renaissance now found expression in the scientific realm, forever altering the course of human knowledge and shaping the foundations of modern science. Thus, the transition from the masterpieces of art to the revolution of science in Italy marked a profound shift in intellectual pursuits and set the stage for a new era of scientific exploration and discovery.

While the Scientific Revolution from 1543 to 1687 CE is often associated with the advancements made in countries like England, France, and Germany, Italy also played a significant role in this transformative period.

One of the prominent figures of this era was Galileo Galilei, the Italian physicist, mathematician, and astronomer. His groundbreaking work in astronomy included his ardent support for the heliocentric model of the solar system. Though this challenged traditional scientific beliefs, his work profoundly impacted the understanding of the natural world. Another notable

Italian figure of the Scientific Revolution was Giambattista Vico, a philosopher and historian. Vico's influential work *New Science* proposed a new approach to understanding history and human civilization, emphasizing the importance of empirical evidence and rejecting purely speculative reasoning.

Italian cities, such as Florence and Padua, morphed into centers of scientific activity and thus attracted scholars from across Europe. Universities in Italy fostered an environment conducive to scientific inquiry, attracting renowned scientists and scholars who made significant contributions to various fields. Becoming a magnet for scientific luminaries, the University of Padua was home to Andreas Vesalius, whose revolutionary work in human anatomy transformed the field of medicine. The city's emphasis on empirical observation and the pursuit of knowledge contributed to the flourishing of scientific disciplines. The achievements and contributions of Italian scholars during the Scientific Revolution expanded the frontiers of knowledge and set the stage for the subsequent development of modern scientific methodology and thinking.

It should be evident that Italy offered much to Europe's cultural, artistic, social, economic, and political growth. For a collection of disparate city-states, it influenced the trajectory of European history much more extensively than its geographic reach. However, as the 17th century CE wore on, bigger powers were coalescing in the continent that far outstripped the resources of Italy's fractured landscape. They had wealth and natural resources, to be sure, but it was not the same as the immense growth that empire nations like Spain, France, and England were beginning to exhibit.

With the economic decline that came alongside their downward trend in European trading power, Italy's various city-states continued to be dragged in and out of the continent's various social, political, and military conflicts. The Thirty Years' War (1618–1648 CE) significantly impacted Italy, although the direct involvement of Italian states varied throughout the conflict.

This war was devastating and primarily fought within the Holy Roman Empire. Aside from the Italian city-states, it involved many European powers, including the well-connected Habsburg family, who controlled the Holy Roman Empire, Spain, and the Spanish Netherlands. Also involved were various Protestant German States, France, Sweden, the Kingdom of Denmark-Norway, and the crowns of England and Scotland. It was mainly a religious conflict between Protestants and Catholics that spiraled out of control.

Italy was, as has been well documented, a fragmented region consisting of numerous independent states and city-states. Various powerful European families could and did claim ownership over these regions at different times. One example is the dueling French and Spanish claims to the Kingdom of Naples. During the Thirty Years' War, many of the northern Italian regions were vassal states of the Holy Roman Empire, so it was practically impossible for city-states like Tuscany and Mantua not to become embroiled in the war. Changing alliances and conflicts throughout the war further intensified the internal divisions within Italy.

The Italian peninsula became a battleground for foreign powers involved in the war. Armies from Spain, France, Austria, and other European states moved across Italian territories, clashing at sites like Tornavento and wreaking havoc on local populations. The widespread destruction, pillaging, and loss of life characteristic of the Thirty Years' War was undoubtedly felt in Italy.

The military presence and the destruction caused by the conflict further disrupted trade routes, agricultural production, and commerce, so Italian states already under strain from a changing world suffered from increased economic decline thanks to the fighting. However, it is important to note that the impact of the

Thirty Years' War on Italy was not uniform across the region, as different states experienced varying degrees of involvement and consequences. Nonetheless, the war contributed to the overall instability, political realignments, and economic challenges faced by Italy during the 17th century CE.

Just a little over fifty years after the conclusion of the Thirty Years' War, another bloody conflict enveloped Europe. The War of the Spanish Succession (1701–1714 CE) was driven by the question of who exactly would succeed the childless Charles II of Spain (r. 1665–1700 CE) to the Spanish throne. The war, which involved multiple nations and kingdoms, reshuffled the balance of power on the continent.

In brief, the leading contenders were Philip of Anjou, a grandson of King Louis XIV of France (r. 1643–1715 CE), who was supported, naturally, by France and its allies, and Archduke Charles of Austria, supported by a coalition that included England, the Dutch Republic, and several German states. Battles and sieges raged across Europe, taking place in Spain, Italy, the Holy Roman Empire, and the Low Countries (present-day Belgium, Luxembourg, and the Netherlands).

Though the war seemed to be fought for the Spanish crown on the surface, there was a deeper purpose. All the rulers of Europe were interested in preventing the consolidation of power by a single dominant state. The ever-shifting and delicate balance of power on the continent was a central concern as countries sought to curtail the expansionist ambitions of France under Louis XIV. With such consequences, it is no surprise that the conflict involved the participation of numerous European powers, including England, France, Spain, the Holy Roman Empire, the Dutch Republic, Portugal, and various German states.

When the Treaty of Utrecht was signed in 1713 CE, it established a compromise whereby Philip of Anjou gained the Spanish throne, becoming King Philip V (r. 1700–1746 CE), but renounced any claim to the French crown. The treaty also resulted in a reorganization of multiple territorial and colonial holdings. The primary winner was England, which gained regions such as Gibraltar that aided its ascendency over the seas.

After the War of the Spanish Succession subsided, the Italian peninsula was a patchwork of duchies controlled mainly by larger European powers. Only a few genuinely independent city-states remained. The subsuming of various regions of Italy into larger empires was not new. After all, the tug of war between the French Angevins and the Spanish Aragonese had played out on the Italian peninsula during the medieval period. Just before the War of the Spanish

Succession, Spain had controlled, either directly or indirectly, the majority of the peninsula, including the large southern kingdoms of Naples and Sicily. Even states that had maintained independence, like Venice, still relied on protection from the much larger Spanish Empire.

However, the map of Italy shifted again with the investiture of Philip of Anjou on the Spanish throne. The newly established Spanish House of Bourbon (with deep familial ties to the French Bourbons) had supplanted a historically Habsburg kingdom, and the Austrian Habsburgs were uneasy. Naturally, Italy, with its strategic location and political ties to various European royal entities, could not avoid the fallout from the war.

Chief among these consequences, as mentioned above, were various territorial rearrangements, most of which were a blow to Spanish holdings. Further treaties to end the war—the Treaty of Rastatt and the Treaty of Baden—awarded the Spanish Netherlands (modern-day Belgium and Luxembourg, among other regions) to the Holy Roman Empire and recognized the emperor's right to rule over the formerly Spanish-controlled Italian states of Milan, Tuscany, Naples, and Sardinia. The Duke of Savoy (part of present-day France) gained Sicily from the Spaniards, though five years later, he would hand it over to the Austrian Habsburgs in exchange for Sardinia.

So with the Spanish largely expelled from the Italian peninsula, the power dynamics looked drastically different than they had for at least the last century. The Austrian Habsburgs now held the old Spanish territories in Italy, which was, in effect, a large percentage of the peninsula. However, the Kingdom of Naples would only fall under their influence for two brief decades. During the War of the Polish Succession (1733–1735 CE), in 1734 CE, Prince Don Carlos de Borbón (Charles of Bourbon), the son of King Philip V of Spain, conquered both Naples and Sicily, bringing the region back under Spanish influence. However, this time it was under the leadership of the Spanish House of Bourbon.

In the central portion of the peninsula lay the Papal States under the authority of the pope. He maintained control over central Italy, including regions such as Latium (Lazio), Umbria, and Marche. Tracking further north, the area was divided by the Duchy of Savoy, Austrian Habsburg holdings, and the still-independent Republic of Venice. Milan floated in and out of Austrian influence throughout the early part of the century. After the War of the Austrian Succession (1740–1748 CE), it remained in their grasp until the dissolution of the Holy Roman Empire in 1806 CE. As for the Spanish, they had managed to claw back the duchies of Parma and Piacenza in 1731 CE.

Aside from territorial shuffling, Italy had a general spirit of reform afoot during the 18th century. This was due, in large part, to the spirit of the Enlightenment, which brought a wave of reform and intellectual awakening to Italy. Deeply influenced by the ideas of French Enlightenment thinkers such as Voltaire, Montesquieu, and Rousseau, Italian intellectuals and rulers embraced the principles of reason, individual freedom, and progress.

Outdated and arbitrary legal systems were called into question, with prominent jurists like the Milanese Cesare Beccaria advocating for the abolition of torture and the establishment of fair and human criminal justice systems based on rational principles. Enlightened rulers and educators also recognized the importance of an informed and enlightened citizenry. A good education was necessary to achieve this, and institutions such as the University of Turin and the University of Padua underwent reforms to modernize the curriculum and promote critical thinking.

Unfortunately for Italy, these reforms were not enough for their respective economies to fully recover after the slump of the 1600s CE. There were brief periods of growth, but the various succession wars coupled with a nasty famine in the 1760s CE denied the Italian states the same rate of growth seen in other parts of the European continent at this time. Furthermore, though the population did grow throughout the century, the rest of the continent's population grew at a rate double Italy's. The stagnation kept the kind of agricultural and industrial revolution seen in nations like England and France at bay. Furthermore, the nobility was eager to hold on to their land, power, and prestige and saw these new reformist ideas threatening their traditional way of life.

Life was getting harder for the average Italian. A region that had once exported many finished goods suddenly became a net importer and only exported cheaper raw materials or partially finished items. Work opportunities were scarcer with a contracting economy, and what had been a slight difference between the northern portion of the peninsula and the southern half split into a wider chasm. To the north, urban industries could survive in smaller villages and the countryside, but in the south, the population came to rely solely on agriculture.

Despite these hardships, political and religious reforms continued to wind their way into Italy. The Catholic Church and the Papal States, with their massive wealth, powerful influence over the populace, and general immunity from secular legislation, were of particular interest to the political thinkers of the Enlightenment. Intellectuals like Beccaria and Pietro Giannone advocated separating church and state, denouncing the Church's political influence and calling for religious tolerance. They argued against the Church's control over education, censorship of ideas, and suppression of scientific inquiry. These critiques resonated strongly in Italy and laid the groundwork for subsequent religious reforms and the later unification of the peninsula.

These ideas reached the respective leaders of Europe's large royal families like the Bourbons and the Habsburgs. As a result, the cadet branches of these families that controlled Italy, like the Habsburg-Lorraines in Milan and the Bourbons in Naples, were among the first to make various political reforms in Italy, mainly during the second half of the 18th century CE.

Milan underwent significant political reforms to modernize its governance and promote greater participation in political affairs. Under the leadership of enlightened rulers like the Holy Roman Empress Maria Theresa (r. 1740–1780), these reforms included the abolition of the corrupt practice of selling offices, the founding of a public bank, the establishment of a more structured administrative system, and the promotion of economic development through policies that encouraged trade and industry. She also initiated a cadastral survey to map out the entirety of the Holy Roman Empire, Milan included.

As for Naples, the rule of King Charles VII (r. 1734–1759) and his successors aimed to modernize the administration, improve governance, and promote economic development. The city was also a hub for Enlightenment thought, welcoming cutting-edge intellectuals like Ferdinando Galiani and Antonio Genovesi. The presence of these philosophers and economists and the new reforms enacted by the government brought Naples closer to the ideals of the Enlightenment by fostering progress and improving the overall quality of life for the Neopolitan people.

The intense focus on intellectual life in the 18th century dovetailed neatly with the rise of Neoclassical art. In Italy, it gained popularity during the latter half of the century as a reaction against the ornate and extravagant style of the previously discussed Baroque and equally elaborate Rococo periods. Inspired by the revival of interest in ancient Greek and Roman art, Neoclassical artists in Italy sought to capture the ideals of harmony, simplicity, and rationality. They drew upon classical themes, mythology, and historical events to create works characterized by clean lines, restrained colors, and a focus on precision and clarity. Artists such as Antonio Canova and Luigi Valadier became renowned for their neoclassical sculptures and decorative arts, drawing inspiration from their Roman forefathers and leaving a lasting legacy of timeless elegance and a renewed appreciation for the classical heritage of Italian art.

Europe was poised for a major change as the Enlightenment reached its zenith. Indeed, a seismic shift was on the horizon, and a charismatic figure was prepared to capitalize on the moment. The rise of Napoleon Bonaparte, a visionary leader and military genius, would soon bring forth a time of tumultuous transformation. With the French Revolution as its catalyst, the Napoleonic era would challenge established powers, redraw borders, and launch a period of modernity across the Italian states.

6

CONQUEST TO UNITY: NAPOLEON AND THE ITALIAN UNIFICATION (1789–1902 CE)

The first ripples of a unified Italy began well before the Risorgimento took place. To the north in France, a revolution erupted in 1789 CE, fueled by ideals of liberty, equality, and fraternity. The violence and bloodshed with which the French people upended their *ancien régime* sent shockwaves throughout Europe as nations began to sprout from kingdoms. The Italian peninsula, too, was swept up in this revolutionary fervor. The winds of change brought by the French Revolution resonated with the aspirations of the Italian people that the Enlightenment ignited. It is no accident that Italy's patriotic red, white, and green colors began appearing around this time. The presence of a foreign invader further spurred this new wave of nationalism.

Napoleon Bonaparte, an enigmatic figure who emerged amidst the turmoil of the French Revolution, came to dominate the European stage around this time. Rising from humble origins on the French island of Corsica, Napoleon's meteoric ascent to power saw him transform France into a formidable military and political force. His ambition and charismatic leadership propelled him to the newly created role of First Consul and later Emperor of the French. With a grand vision of reshaping Europe according to his design, Napoleon embarked on a series of military campaigns to reshape the continent's political landscape.

Italy, in particular, found itself inexorably linked to Napoleon's ambitions. The Italian peninsula, divided into multiple states and under the control of foreign powers, presented an enticing target for Napoleon's expansionist agenda. Inspired by the ideals of the French Revolution, he sought to dismantle the old order represented by hereditary nobility and establish a new order based on meritocracy and national unity. Through military conquest, diplomatic maneuvers, and alliances with Italian revolutionaries, Napoleon brought about profound changes in Italy, setting the stage for the eventual unification of the Italian states. When the age of Napoleon dawned, Italy stood poised at a threshold of a transformative era.

Napoleon's interest in Italy can be attributed to several factors. Firstly, Italy's strategic location and rich cultural heritage made it an appealing target for conquest. Its position in the Mediterranean at the crossroads of Europe made it a gateway to other territories, allowing Napoleon to expand his influence and consolidate power. Italy's history as the birthplace of the Roman Empire and the Renaissance and its renowned artistic and intellectual legacy held a strong allure for Napoleon, who saw himself as a new Caesar, a patron of the arts, and a promoter of Enlightenment ideals.

Furthermore, Italy's fragmented political landscape handed Napoleon the perfect opportunity to establish French dominance by exploiting existing rivalries and simultaneously ousting one of his geopolitical rivals—the entrenched Austrians. The Italian states had changed hands so many times over the years. Napoleon believed a unified Italy aligned with the principles of the French Revolution, notably nationalism and popular sovereignty, would be appreciated throughout the peninsula.

Moreover, Italy offered valuable resources and economic opportunities. The region was historically known for its agricultural productivity, vibrant trade networks, and wealthy merchant cities. By gaining control over Italy, Napoleon aimed to secure these economic advantages and leverage them to support his ambitious military and political endeavors.

Napoleon's first campaign into Italy in 1796 CE during the War of the First Coalition (1792–1797 CE) marked the beginning of his extraordinary military career and set the stage for subsequent conquests. He led the French army and launched a daring and innovative offensive against the Austrian forces controlling northern Italy. Napoleon employed swift and decisive maneuvers, utilizing rapid marches, flanking movements, and concentrated attacks to outmaneuver and defeat his adversaries.

His victories at the battles of Montenotte, Millesimo, and Lodi showcased his tactical brilliance and earned him the admiration of his troops. The Italian population, weary of foreign domination and inspired by the ideals of the French Revolution, initially welcomed Napoleon as a liberator. With their support, he established new republican governments in northern Italy, dismantling the existing structures and promoting reforms such as religious tolerance, the abolition of feudal practices, and the introduction of the Napoleonic Code, a civil law code he designed.

Napoleon's campaign in Italy secured significant territorial gains for France and laid the groundwork for his larger vision of a unified Italy. Through diplomatic maneuvering, he compelled various Italian states to join his cause, gradually eroding the influence of foreign powers. Yet at the same time, Napoleon ultimately believed that France (controlled by himself, of course) was more suited to govern Italy than the Italians themselves. This eventually caused tension and friction between the two parties.

However, he was unsatisfied with solely northern Italy and turned his sights southward. His campaigns continued in central Italy from 1797 to 1799 CE, and the ambitious French general made his presence felt throughout the peninsula. One of the pivotal turning points occurred during the Battle of Rivoli in 1797 CE, where Napoleon showcased his military mind and achieved a resounding victory against the Austrian forces.

Eager to extend French influence, Napoleon skillfully negotiated the Treaty of Campo Formio the same year, formally concluding the War of the First Coalition. This landmark agreement marked a significant redrawing of the political landscape in Italy, recognizing French control over Lombardy while ceding Venetian territories and the city of Venice to Austria. This act brought a stunning ten centuries of independent Venetian rule to a close. Quickly flexing his new power over portions of the peninsula, Napoleon founded the Cisalpine Republic, a French-backed state in northern Italy that embraced the ideals of the French Revolution.

Napoleon directed his attention south toward the Papal States in his pursuit of even greater dominion. Though short-lived, the occupation of Rome in 1798 CE and the establishment of a Roman Republic (1798–1799 CE) were symbolic gestures that shook the foundations of the region. The pope's temporal authority was diminished, making way for the later attrition of papal power in the 1800s CE.

Amidst his seemingly endless military conquests, one momentous battle stood out: the Battle of Marengo in 1800 CE during the War of the Second Coalition (1798–1802 CE). Napoleon's strategic brilliance was on full display as he secured a slim victory over the Austrian forces, consolidating French control in northern and central Italy. This triumph not only bolstered Napoleon's position but also played a pivotal role in the downfall of the Holy Roman Empire and the shaping of Italy's political landscape.

By the turn of the 19th century CE, Napoleon had become the First Consul of France and was in firm control of the French Republic and all its territories, including Italy. Under Napoleon's rule, Italy underwent a series of political and administrative transformations. In 1802 CE, he established the Italian Republic, a satellite state of France, encompassing territories in northern and central Italy, but his ambitions in Italy did not stop there.

By 1805 CE, he declared himself King of Italy, bestowing himself with the Iron Crown of Lombardy, a medieval relic with a murky, potentially Byzantine origin. This act further solidified his control over the region. It enhanced his legitimacy as a ruler, though it did make him seem less like a champion of the people and much more like the kind of autocratic foreign monarch Italy had seen many times before.

During this period, Napoleon continued to launch military campaigns to expand French control in Italy, facing opposition from various European states, particularly the Third Coalition formed by Austria, Russia, Sweden, the United Kingdom, Naples, and Sicily. However, Napoleon's military prowess kept him in the lead with several victories, the most notable being the Battle of Austerlitz in 1805 CE, which secured French dominance and played a part in the demise of the Holy Roman Empire.

Napoleon's presence in Italy brought about significant changes across different aspects of society. He continued to introduce sweeping reforms, including

legal and administrative changes, economic modernization, and infrastructure development. These reforms
aimed to centralize power, stimulate economic growth,
and strengthen the region's ties to the French Empire.
While these may have benefitted the peninsula, Italian
citizens were beginning to sour towards him. Some still
saw him as a liberator who embodied the ideals of the
French Revolution, but others resented foreign occupation and yearned for true Italian independence.

Aware of his fluctuating popularity, Napoleon established satellite states in Italy to cement his control.
These included the Kingdom of Italy, which encompassed territories in northern and central Italy, and the
Kingdom of Naples, governed first by Napoleon's
brother Joseph Bonaparte and later by his brother-in-
law, Joachim Murat. These puppet states aligned with
French interests and continued to implement reforms
inspired by the French Revolution.

Italy was divided into three portions—the northern-
most part of the peninsula, which was annexed into the
French Empire; some northern and central states that
were joined to create the newly minted Kingdom of
Italy; and the southern Kingdom of Naples. The Papal
States were largely left alone since Napoleon retained a
somewhat cordial relationship with Pope Pius VII (r.
18001823 CE). After all, the same pope crowned him

Emperor of France in 1804 CE, lending an air of religious legitimacy to his new monarchy. However, when Napoleon invaded the Papal States five years later, he imprisoned Pope Pius VII and annexed his territories. The pontiff's lands were returned to him after Napoleon's fall in 1814 CE. As for Venice, the Austrians ceded control to Napoleon after the Battle of Austerlitz, though like the Papal States, Venice would be returned to Austrian rule after 1814 CE.

While Napoleon's rule brought some benefits, such as infrastructure development and administrative efficiency, it also resulted in challenges and resistance. The introduction of conscription for the French army stirred discontent among the Italian population, leading to resentment and resistance against foreign occupation. The heavy taxation imposed to fund Napoleon's military campaigns also strained the Italian economy and contributed to popular discontent.

Napoleon's power began to wane in the early 19th century CE. With his decline, Italy soon became a battleground, with European powers circling like vultures over the scraps of the French Empire. The Congress of Vienna in 1815 CE marked the end of Napoleon's rule in Italy, as the region was redivided among various powers, including Austria and the smaller Kingdom of Sardinia.

Despite Napoleon's eventual defeat and the re-establishment of foreign control in Italy, his influence left a lasting impact on the region. The Napoleonic reforms, particularly the legal and administrative changes, laid the groundwork for future developments in Italy, including the fight for Italian independence and the coming Risorgimento.

The Italian Risorgimento, meaning "resurgence" or "rebirth," refers to the 19th-century CE movement for Italian unification and independence. It took many different events and nearly sixty years to come to fruition, but the Congress of Vienna was a catalyzing event. After Napoleon's defeat, the larger European powers who had a hand in his downfall redrew that map of Europe to favor their sociopolitical aims. These nations, primarily Great Britain, Austria, Russia, and Prussia, were governed by monarchs and were eager to put down any revolutionary sentiment that lingered inside and outside their kingdoms. Though Napoleon, in the end, was no great champion of representative government, the years leading up to and during his reign had been decidedly turbulent for Europe's monarchies.

However, the cat was out of the bag, and it would be impossible for the European royal families to return to their heyday of absolutist rule. It was twilight for these kings and queens, but they did not quite know it yet. In 1820 CE, the first of several revolutionary sparks lit on the continent. A revolt in Cádiz, Spain, led to the establishment of the Constitution of Cádiz, which later served as a framework for Italian patriots.

One year later, Italian revolutionaries began to call for a constitution. This had limited success, and the Kingdom of Two Sicilies (formerly the Kingdom of Naples) and the Kingdom of Sardinia gained constitutions. Unfortunately, though, these gains were short-lived, and with the Austrian military's aid, the full power of the monarchs of both kingdoms was restored.

In the 1830s CE, several uprisings ignited across the Italian states, inspired by nationalist sentiments and the continued spread of liberal ideals throughout Europe. These rebellions, such as the revolutions in Modena, Parma, and the Papal States, aimed to challenge foreign dominion over the peninsula and establish independent Italian states.

Two key figures of the Risorgimento must be quickly discussed before proceeding: Giuseppe Mazzini and Giuseppe Garibaldi. As an influential nationalist and political activist, Mazzini fervently advocated for a unified and independent Italy. He co-founded the secret society known as Young Italy in 1831 CE, which aimed to promote Italian unity, republican ideals, and popular participation in the political process. Mazzini's impassioned writings and powerful oratory inspired countless Italians to join the cause and fight for their nation's liberation.

As for Garibaldi, he is remembered as a legendary figure in Italian history whose name remains synonymous with the spirit of the Risorgimento. Known as the "Hero of Two Worlds," he was a skilled military leader and a passionate advocate for Italian independence. He led several successful campaigns, most notably the famous Expedition of the Thousand in 1860 CE, which will be discussed shortly. With his volunteer army, known as the Redshirts, Garibaldi conquered the Kingdom of the Two Sicilies, playing a crucial part in tying southern Italy to the northern regions.

In 1848 CE, another wave of revolutions swept Europe, including Italy. The uprisings marked a significant turning point in the Risorgimento. Revolts erupted in various Italian states, demanding liberal reforms, constitutional governments, and national unity. Notable events during this period include the Sicilian uprising and the establishment of another Roman Republic under the leadership of Mazzini and Garibaldi.

The Sicilian Revolution of 1848 CE marked a pivotal moment in the struggle for Italian independence and the broader context of European revolutionary movements. Sparked by widespread discontent with Bourbon rule, Sicilians rose against their oppressive rulers and demanded political and social reforms. The revolution was somewhat of a populist movement, with Sicilian civilians taking up arms and forming a provisional government. Their goals included the establishment of a constitutional monarchy and the unification of Sicily with the rest of Italy. Although Bourbon forces eventually suppressed the revolution, it served as a precursor to the broader wave of revolutions and upheavals that swept across Europe later.

During the same year, Rome became a stage for significant political change. After the Papal Minister, Pellegrino Rossi, was assassinated, Pope Pius IX (r. 18461878 CE) fled Rome, and the Roman Republic was founded. Inspired by nationalist sentiments and dissatisfaction with foreign rule, Roman citizens and other Italian revolutionaries took to the streets demanding reforms and independence from the papal authority.

With Mazzini and Garibaldi leading the way, this new Roman Republic aimed to establish a government based on republican principles, with a constitution and elected officials. However, the republic faced numerous challenges, including opposition from conservative forces and military interventions by foreign powers. By

1850, the Republic was no more. Despite its short-lived existence, it became a powerful symbol of the Italian people's aspirations for self-determination. It laid the groundwork for future efforts toward Italian unification and the later dissolution of the Papal States. Twenty years later, Pope Pius IX would be the last Catholic pope to rule as a secular monarch; beyond the walls of Vatican City, all of his successors would be relegated to spiritual authority alone.

Despite the impressive ground gained by revolutionary forces, it was not yet the hour for Italy's independence. Harsh repression from conservative troops and foreign intervention, particularly from the French and the Austrians, pushed back against the work of leaders like Mazzini and Garibaldi. However, the momentum of the Risorgimento could not be stopped.

A new figure emerged in Sardinia—Camillo Benso, Count of Cavour (Count Camillo Benso di Cavour), was a prominent figure in the Italian Risorgimento and played a vital role in the unification of Italy. Known for his political acumen and diplomatic skills, Cavour served as the Prime Minister of the Kingdom of Sardinia, a leading state in the Italian peninsula. Rather than the broad militaristic approach favored by revolutionaries like Garibaldi and Mazzini, Cavour pursued a more strategic approach to consolidate alliances and exploit international rivalries to advance the cause of Italian unity.

He presented the continual skirmishes in Italy as a diplomatic problem for the rest of the European continent, hoping to use Emperor Napoleon III's (r. 18521870 CE) French Empire to squeeze the Austrians out of the peninsula. His canny diplomacy and calculated actions were pivotal in the unification process.

Though he and Cavour held the same goal, Garibaldi grew frustrated with the slow pace of diplomatic machinations. In 1860 CE, another revolt broke out in Sicily against their Bourbon rulers. Garibaldi, eager to capitalize on the unrest, embarked on an ambitious military campaign known as the "Expedition of the Thousand" or the "Expedition of the Redshirts."

The essential aim of the enterprise was to liberate the Kingdom of the Two Sicilies, which encompassed the regions of southern Italy and Sicily, from Bourbon rule and unite it with Cavour's Kingdom of Sardinia. Garibaldi and his volunteer Redshirt army of about a thousand men launched from the port of Quarto near Genoa and sailed for Sicily, where they landed at Marsala in May 1860 CE.

The Redshirts quickly gained support from the local population as they marched through the island, easily defeating the Bourbon forces in several battles. Their military successes and Garibaldi's charismatic leadership fueled a groundswell of popular support, with volunteers joining their ranks as they advanced. After securing Sicily, Garibaldi proclaimed himself the island's dictator in the name of the current king of Sardinia, King Victor Emmanuel II (r. 18491878 CE).

With Sicily now mastered, Garibaldi did not stop. Instead, his forces crossed the Strait of Messina and marched into mainland Italy, where they encountered minimal resistance. Inspiring widespread enthusiasm and uprisings among the local population, Garibaldi was viewed as a champion of Italian independence and unity. As a result, when they moved northward, Garibaldi's forces grew significantly in numbers, swelling to around 20,000 volunteers. The campaign culminated at the Battle of Volturno in October 1860 CE, where Garibaldi's forces defeated the Bourbon army.

However, after Volturno, Garibaldi marched no further. Cavour, who had been mostly supportive of the Expedition of the Thousand in the beginning, feared that it was deteriorating into a populist fervor. As a result, King Victor Emmanuel II and his forces met Garibaldi and his Thousand outside of Rome, halting their progress before they moved on to the crown jewel of the peninsula, which was under French protection at the time. Once Garibaldi turned the regions he had successfully liberated over to Victor Emmanuel, all of Italy except Rome and Venetia (Venice and the surrounding lands) was pulled under the crown of Sardinia.

With the Kingdom of the Two Sicilies annexed to the Kingdom of Sardinia under the leadership of King Victor Emmanuel II, the dream of Italian unification was closer than ever. The following year, in 1861 CE, Italy was officially proclaimed a united kingdom with King Victor Emmanuel II at its head. Venetia continued under Austrian governance, and Rome remained under papal control.

Five years later, an opportunity for Venice's incorporation into the Kingdom of Italy arose during the Austro-Prussian War of 1866 CE. Italy, now led by Prime Minister Alfonso Ferrero La Marmora, formed an alliance with Prussia against Austria, likely realizing that the war gave Italy a golden opportunity to reclaim territories under Austrian control. La Marmora's gamble paid off when Prussia emerged victorious, and the Treaty of Vienna in 1866 granted Venetia to Italy. This territorial acquisition was met with joy and celebration among the Italian population, as it represented the fulfillment of a long-held desire to reunite historically significant regions with the rest of Italy. Venice's rich cultural heritage, artistic legacy, and strategic importance further enhanced the symbolic and practical significance of its incorporation.

Yet, Rome remained outside of Italian control. The Papal States, which included Rome, were still under the rule of Pope Pius IX and protected by French troops stationed in the city. However, French troops were needed on their home soil during the Franco-Prussian War (18701871 CE), and Rome was left vulnerable to Italian forces. In response, Italian soldiers under the command of General Raffaele Cadorna advanced toward Rome. On September 20, 1870, they breached the city's defenses, claiming Rome for Italy and ending secular papal rule.

Unlike Venice, Rome's addition to the Kingdom of Italy was met with mixed reactions. Supporters of Italian unification celebrated the event as the final step towards a united Italy, fulfilling a long-held aspiration. Still, in a majority Catholic nation like Italy, the loss of Rome and the Papal States was a significant blow to the papacy and the Catholic Church.

Following the incorporation of Rome, the Italian government declared the city the capital of the Kingdom of Italy, solidifying Rome's status as the political, administrative, and cultural heart of the newly unified Italian state. The long-dreamed goals of the Risorgimento were realized at last.

Now with the entire territory of the peninsula unified, the Kingdom of Italy entered a period of consolidation and further development to establish itself as a nation. Victor Emmanuel II and his successors worked with the government to develop a stable political system focused on solidifying its authority, implementing administrative reforms, and strengthening state institutions.

But challenges persisted. Regional disparities, particularly between the industrialized north and the agrarian south, posed ongoing socio-economic issues. Social tensions, labor disputes, and political divisions arose as Italy transitioned from a collection of independent states into a unified nation.

Internationally, Italy sought to solidify its position on the global stage. Eager to catch up with other European powers, it engaged in colonial expansion, acquiring territories in Africa and the Mediterranean. They gained Eritrea in 1882 CE, Somalia in 1889 CE, and Libya in 1911 CE. These overseas ventures aimed to bolster Italy's prestige and influence but added to the complexities of managing an empire.

As Italy approached the 20th century, its prime minister, Giovanni Giolitti, powerfully shaped the country. Both loved and reviled, Giolitti was one of the longest-serving prime ministers in Italian history and a pivotal figure in the shaping of modern Italy. He was committed to modernization and economic progress, implementing policies to stimulate industrial growth and improve the country's economy. Giolitti promoted free trade, encouraged foreign investments, and initiated infrastructure projects to enhance transportation and communication networks. His economic reforms played a crucial role in transforming Italy into an industrialized nation, particularly in the northern regions, where industrial centers flourished.

Giolitti also sought to address social issues and improve the welfare of the working class. He introduced labor reforms that protected workers' rights, regulated working hours, and improved working conditions. Giolitti's policies helped mitigate labor disputes and fostered a more stable social climate.

Furthermore, Giolitti played a significant role in advancing the cause of parliamentary democracy and political stability. His pragmatic approach to politics involved forming coalitions and seeking compromise among political factions. Giolitti emphasized the importance of consensus and worked towards expanding suffrage, making elections more inclusive, and strengthening democratic institutions.

However, Giolitti's political career was not without controversy. Though responsible for bringing Italy prosperity, Giolitti had his fair share of enemies and is remembered for holding onto power through less-than-moral means. His practice of using personal hand-shake deals, corruption, and violence to achieve election results has come to be known as *giolittisimo*. These issues tarnished his reputation and created divisions among his supporters and opponents.

Outside of Italy's growing sense of self, in the early 20th century CE, Europe was teetering ever closer to an explosion. It was an odd time of transition where traditional kingdoms still existed alongside modern nation-states, and old alliances faced many shifts and challenges. Italy had historically been aligned with Germany and Austria-Hungary as part of the Triple Alliance formed in 1882 CE, and this served Italy by maintaining stability and protecting Italian territorial ambitions. However, as tensions in Europe escalated, Italy realized strategic choices had to be made in place of honoring historical obligations.

Italy thus entered into a delicate balancing act. While formally allied with Germany and Austria-Hungary, Italy maintained reservations about their aggressive territorial aspirations. The Irredentist movement in Italy was particularly critical of Italy's continued adherence to the Triple Alliance. Fervent nationalists who had advocated for the reunification of Italian-speaking territories, the Italian Irredentists disregarded the constraints of the Triple Alliance and prioritized Italian territorial ambitions. Of particular importance were the regions of Trentino, Trieste, and Istria, which were in Austro-Hungarian clutches. The Irredentist movement challenged Italy's foreign policy, as it fueled internal pressures and demands for territorial expansion that directly opposed the obligations and commitments of the Triple Alliance.

So, what alternatives were available if Italy would not stay loyal to the Triple Alliance? In 1902 CE, Italy signed a secret defensive pact with France, the Franco-Italian Agreement. This agreement aimed to secure French support in Italy's pursuit of territorial gains in the event of a conflict with Austria-Hungary. The French agreed to back Italian claims on Libya in exchange for Italy's support of French assertions in Morocco. Most importantly, it demonstrated Italy's willingness to pursue its present national interests over its historical alliance commitments.

However, Europe was a tinderbox, and Italy's careful balancing act was becoming impossible to maintain.

Though now a unified country, the oncoming century would bring untold violence and conflict to Italy at home and abroad. Looming on the horizon was the gathering storm of World War I (1914–1918 CE), which would test Italy's alliances, ambitions, and resilience. As the world plunged into this cataclysmic conflict, Italy faced critical decisions that shaped its destiny and tested its aspirations for territorial expansion and international prominence. The Risorgimento had laid the groundwork, and now Italy stood as one nation on the precipice, ready to face the challenges and uncertainties of the turbulent times ahead.

7

THE CRUELEST CENTURY: ITALY ENTERS THE AGE OF MODERNITY (1914–1980 CE)

W hen Archduke Franz Ferdinand slumped forward in his car on June 28, 1914 CE, Europe's carefully constructed balance of power collapsed into total calamity. Alliances were called upon, and soon all of the major nations of Europe were at each other's throats. Incensed by the slaying of their crown prince, Austria-Hungary looked to Germany to support their war against Serbia. Serbia turned to Imperial Russia, who, in turn, reached out to France. Gavrilo Princip's bullet started a regional conflict, quickly spiraling out of control into a global war.

At the outset of World War I, there was the old Triple Alliance of Austria-Hungary, Germany, and Italy. However, Italy chose not to honor the agreement and instead remained neutral. Bulgaria and the Ottoman

Empire also entered the fray on the side of Austria-Hungary, and together the four nations formed the Central Powers. On the other side was Serbia, backed by the Allied Powers of Russia, France, Great Britain, Japan, and later, Italy and the United States.

The challenging decision to opt for neutrality in the early days of World War I was controversial but not one that would last very long. Instead, Italian leaders saw an opportunity to renegotiate territorial claims and potentially expand their influence by joining the side that offered the most advantageous terms. In 1915 CE, Italy entered the war on the side of the Allies after signing the Treaty of London, which promised territorial gains at the expense of Austria-Hungary.

Soon, the Italian front became a significant theater of war, with intense fighting in the mountainous regions along the Austro-Italian border. The rugged terrain presented substantial challenges to both sides, and the front line spanned the length of the Alps, from the Adriatic Sea in the east to the Swiss border in the west. Steep mountains, deep valleys, and harsh weather conditions made military operations extremely fraught.

Under General Luigi Cadorna's command, Italian forces launched several offensives to break through the Austro-Hungarian lines and seize control of strategic positions. However, progress was slow and costly due to the challenging mountainous terrain and the formidable defensive posts held by the enemy. Furthermore, history has not been kind to Cadorna and his tactics. His Austro-Hungarian opponent, General Svetozar Boroević von Bojna, routinely outmatched him.

Boroević skillfully utilized the natural advantages of the terrain to mount a strong defense. Though the Western Front is remembered for trench warfare, the Italian Front, or Isonzo Front, was also characterized by a series of trench lines and fortified positions. The geography of the Alps further forced intricate systems of mountain warfare, including artillery, mine warfare, and savage hand-to-hand combat.

The battles along the Italian front were marked by brutal fighting and heavy casualties. Soldiers faced enemy fire, extreme weather conditions, avalanches, landslides, and disease. One of the most significant engagements on the Italian front was the Battle of Caporetto in 1917 CE. The Austro-Hungarian and German forces launched a massive offensive that resulted in a breakthrough, causing the collapse of the Italian line and forcing the Italian army to retreat.

However, the Italian front witnessed a turnaround in 1918 CE. With the support of Allied forces, Italy launched a successful counteroffensive at the Battle of

Vittorio Veneto, which contributed to the collapse of the Austro-Hungarian Empire. On November 3 of the same year, Italy and Austria-Hungary signed the Armistice of Villa Giusti, effectively ending hostilities on the Isonzo Front. This was a massive victory for Italy, granting it control over contested regions like Trentino, South Tyrol, Trieste, Gorizia, and Istria—regions that the Irredentists had wanted to fold into the Kingdom of Italy before the onset of the war.

A little over a week after Villa Giusti, on November 11, the Armistice of Compiègne was signed, bringing World War I to an official close. Naturally, the Italian front had a profound impact on Italy's experience of World War I. It claimed the lives of hundreds of thousands of soldiers, resulted in widespread destruction, and exacerbated social and economic hardships within the country. The harsh realities of war and the sacrifices made by soldiers on the Italian front left a deep chasm within Italy's collective memory and shaped the nation's post-war aspirations and political developments.

After the conclusion of World War I, Italy faced significant challenges across political, economic, and social spheres. The war left a legacy of destruction and disillusionment across Europe, particularly in Italy, with increased political fragmentation and the rise of extremist movements. The nation grappled with economic hardships, including inflation and unemployment, as well as social unrest fueled by veterans' demands and workers' strikes. The post-war period saw a reevaluation of traditional values and the emergence of new cultural movements. These challenges set the stage for further political developments, eventually leading to one Benito Mussolini.

The rise of fascism can be attributed to Italy's aforementioned challenges during the early 20th century CE. Mussolini was a charismatic leader and quickly emerged as the driving force behind the movement. Fascism gained momentum after the horrors of World War I as Italy struggled with social unrest, economic woes, and a general disillusionment with traditional politics.

Founding the National Fascist Party (*Partito Nazionale Fascista* or PNF) in 1921 CE, Mussolini capitalized on nationalistic fervor, anti-communist sentiments, and the palpable fear that led to a desire for strong leadership. The party's ideology emphasized the primacy of the state, exalting national identity and promoting authoritarian rule. Mussolini and his followers promised to restore order and tackle economic and social problems while calling on the historical legacy of ancient Rome to be their guide.

Fascism capitalized on widespread discontent with the liberal democratic system, which was perceived as weak and ineffective. The party employed aggressive propaganda, utilizing mass rallies, paramilitary squads (such as the Blackshirts), and a cult of personality around Mussolini to gain power and suppress opposition.

In 1922 CE, Mussolini marched on Rome, showcasing the power of his supporters. This led to the appointment of Mussolini as prime minister by King Victor Emmanuel III (r. 1900–1946 CE). Once in power, Mussolini quickly consolidated it, dismantling democratic institutions and establishing a one-party dictatorship. Corporatist policies that aimed to bring industry, labor, and agriculture under state control were enacted, and his regime also pursued an aggressive public relations campaign that promoted nationalism, imperialistic ambitions, and the dream of Italy as a world power.

Fascist Italy emphasized totalitarian control, with pervasive censorship, surveillance, and suppression of political opposition. Dissent was stifled, and propaganda was used to shape public opinion and maintain the regime's authority. Mussolini's authoritarian rule directly impacted Italy's involvement in World War II as part of the Axis Powers.

To the north in Germany, after the humiliating defeat in World War I, nationalistic sentiment and a desire for stability drove Adolf Hitler to power. Mussolini, though not necessarily hugely enamored by Hitler personally, was aware of certain ideological affinities the two nations shared. He was also cognizant of Hitler's popularity and somewhat jealous of his success. Mussolini, eager to revive the glory of Rome, believed that allying himself with Nazi Germany and Imperial Japan was the surest route to this goal.

In addition to ideological considerations, strategic and geopolitical interests played a role in Italy's alliance choices. Mussolini sought to expand Italy's influence and territorial possessions, particularly in the Mediterranean. He believed aligning with Germany and Japan would present opportunities for territorial gains, resource access, and increased military power.

Italy formally joined the Axis powers by signing the Pact of Steel in May 1939 CE. This solidified the military and political alliance between Italy and Germany and laid the foundation for their collaboration throughout World War II. Subsequently, Italy's alignment with Japan in the Tripartite Pact of 1940 CE further entrenched its position as an Axis Power. Thus, the same year the Tripartite Pact was signed, Italy entered into World War II against the Allied Powers of

Great Britain, the Soviet Union, France, and later, the United States. Sadly for Italy, their entanglement in this global conflict would prove disastrous for the nation.

Italy's military capabilities were limited compared to its Axis partners, and its armed forces were ill-prepared for the demands of a large-scale war. Still, its involvement in the conflict made fighting in the Mediterranean an absolute reality. Italian military campaigns did not have the same ferocity as their German allies and suffered from strategic errors, logistical challenges, and weak leadership. The invasion of Greece in 1940 CE and the subsequent counteroffensive by Greek and Allied forces resulted in a significant setback for Italy.

However, the main thrust of Italian aggression came under Marshal Rodolfo Graziani in the North Africa campaign from 1940 to 1943 CE. This was primarily waged against British and Commonwealth forces to seize control of Egypt and the Suez Canal and would give Italy a strategic advantage in the Mediterranean and the Middle East. When Graziani failed to achieve the desired results against the British, well-known "Desert Fox" General Erwin Rommel of the German Afrika Korps arrived to take over the floundering Axis cause.

Italian forces were inadequately prepped and often lacked sufficient resources and supplies. The inexperience of their commanders led to tactical errors, and it was easy for the British to hold them off. Rommel's arrival in North Africa in early 1941 CE injected new energy into the Italian-German joint campaign. Under his leadership, the Axis forces launched a series of offensives known as the Desert War, which achieved initial success. They pushed the British Eighth Army back, capturing Tobruk and advancing deep into Egypt.

Eventually, the tide of the campaign turned against the Axis powers, with reinvigorated British forces ultimately pushing them out of North Africa. The Italian troops suffered heavy losses, and the campaign ended in May 1943 with the final surrender of Axis forces in Tunisia.

Aside from the failure in North Africa, Italy suffered setbacks in other theaters of the war that exposed the weaknesses of Mussolini's fascist reign. Internal opposition to Mussolini's leadership grew, and the Italian Fascist Grand Council voted to strip him of his powers. His arrest and subsequent imprisonment marked the end of his regime and the collapse of fascist rule in Italy. Mussolini officially stepped down in July 1943 CE.

Several months after the failure in North Africa, Italy was invaded by the Allied Powers. British and American forces landed near Calabria and began a systematic campaign to liberate Italy from German occupation and dismantle the fascist hold on the nation. The Allies faced solid German resistance, particularly in the mountainous terrain of central Italy, but managed to make gradual progress northward nevertheless.

Five days after the Allies landed, Italy officially surrendered on September 8, 1943 CE, and one month later, Italy declared war on their former partners, joining the side of the Allied powers in the struggle against Hitler. However, the Germans remained entrenched on the peninsula, and the fighting persisted until the eventual liberation of Rome in June 1944. Cognizant of the turning tide and fearful for his safety, on April 28, 1945 CE, Benito Mussolini attempted to flee Italy with his mistress, Clara Petacci. Captured by Italian partisans, they were executed by firing squad the following day. After the execution, their bodies were taken to Milan and hung upside down in the Piazzale Loreto. Subjected to abuse and mutilation by the crowd, Mussolini and Petacci were eventually taken down and buried in an unmarked grave. However, they were later reinterred by their respective families.

After the upheaval faced by Italy in World War II, a period of intense rebuilding and transformation began. The country transitioned from a monarchy to a republic in 1946 CE, and King Umberto II (r. 1946) abdicated as a democratic system was formally established by the will of the people. Though Italy faced numerous challenges, including economic disparities between the northern and southern portions of the nation, political stabilization, corruption, and social reconstruction, the post-war years still witnessed significant industrial growth, urbanization, and the development of a welfare state.

Like many other nations, Italy embarked on a path of reconstruction and modernization. This led to the "Italian Economic Miracle," also known as *Il Boom*, an unprecedented period of economic growth and transformation that rocked Italy during the 1950s and 1960s CE. The country witnessed significant industrial expansion, particularly in manufacturing, automobiles, and fashion. Mass migration from rural areas to urban centers fueled the labor force and contributed to urbanization. The Italian Economic Miracle is one of the major success stories in recent history, raising the quality of life for many Italians. As living standards and consumption rose, a healthy middle class emerged, spurring infrastructural developments, including the construction of highways, factories, and residential buildings.

However, even as the economy progressed, Italy was not immune to the popular beliefs of the 1960s and 1970s CE. Social movements, political protests, and overall cultural shifts were the hallmark of these decades. Among these were student uprisings, labor strikes, and activism that advocated for civil rights, women's rights, and increased political participation. These movements reflected the desire for social justice and an eschewing of traditional values.

Alongside these societal changes, Italy faced political instability, characterized by frequent changes in government and the rise of extremism on both sides of the political spectrum. The country was affected by acts of terrorism. One group, in particular, was the Red Brigades, which carried out high-profile kidnappings and assassinations, like the kidnapping of former prime minister Aldo Moro. This was a period of progressive change and political turmoil, further characterized by an economic slump after the post-war years of prosperity.

The twentieth century was an unbelievable time of maturation for Italy, growing from a disparate collection of states under one crown into a democratic nation with a fully formed national identity. It became a pivotal player on the world stage, fighting in major conflicts and having a decisive impact on the future of the European continent. Towards the end of the twentieth century, Italian culture became a lucrative export for the nation, with designers and fashion houses producing exquisitely made goods that became a hallmark of luxury worldwide. The brand names Armani, Ferrari, Gucci, Lamborghini, Prada, Pucci, and Versace are all Italian and came into existence during the 20th century CE. It was throughout these one hundred years that Italy became the country it is today: a destination for tourism, fashion, gastronomic delights, history, and culture.

8

ITALY TODAY AND TOMORROW (1980–2020S CE)

F ine leather goods. Gorgeous sports cars. Delicious food. Beautiful people. Stunning cities. Delectable wine. These have all been staples of Italian culture for at least the last seventy years. However, though these things are all true, more lurks beneath the surface. In Italian history's dynamic and ever-changing landscape, the period from the 1980s CE to the present is filled with profound transformations, challenges, and triumphs.

This era witnessed Italy navigating a complex web of political, economic, social, and cultural shifts, shaping the nation's identity and trajectory in the modern world. From political scandals to economic reforms, from social movements to technological advancements, the multifaceted story of Italy's journey in recent decades tells a tale of globalization, internal and external pressures, and the fight to redefine its role on the international stage.

After the political movements, terrorism, and economic downturns of the previous decade, the 1980s CE began as a period of economic growth and rampant consumerism. Though the early portion of the decade saw continued violence from left-wing extremist groups like the Red Brigades, the focus was less on political ideology and more on business, money, and the economy. The protests that had been so popular just a few years prior saw less and less turnout as the wider population turned away from political activism. Union membership, election turnout, and political party membership faltered throughout the decade.

Thus, with this elevation of the financial sector and general withdrawal from Italian political concerns came greed, corruption, and scandal. In the early 1990s CE, Italy was rocked by the Tangentopoli Investigations. Known as the "Clean Hands" or *Mani Pulite* operation, these were a series of high-profile corruption investigations that exposed kickbacks, bribes, and embezzlement within the government and the nation's political and business elite. The probe was initiated by a group of prosecutors in Milan led by Antonio Di Pietro, who targeted politicians, officials, and business leaders from across the political spectrum. It reached as high as the former prime minister and head of the Italian Socialist Party, Benedetto "Bettino" Craxi, who would ultimately face multiple political corruption charges.

Though necessary and cleansing, the investigations were detrimental to the Italian political machine and eventually led to the complete unraveling of several major political parties. The Christian Democracy Party became the Italian Popular Party and was relegated to the fringes of political discourse. The Italian Socialist Party, a major political player since the 1960s, was fully dissolved, as was one of its offshoots, the Italian Democratic Socialist Party. The final party to fall was the Italian Liberal Party, which the famed Camillo di Cavour founded in the mid-1800s CE. Naturally, such a shake-up sent shockwaves through Italian society, rattling the foundations of the political establishment and triggering a profound crisis of confidence in the country's institutions.

The Tangentopoli Investigations had a far-reaching impact on society and politics, becoming a watershed moment in Italian history. They highlighted the urgent need for political reform, transparency, and account-ability. While the investigations caused political insta-bility in the short term, they also sparked a wave of anti-corruption measures and institutional reforms to rebuild public trust and restore integrity in Italian politics. The public outcry and power vacuum that followed the scandal contributed to the rise of new political forces, including the formation of the center-right Forza Italia party by media mogul Silvio Berlusconi.

Berlusconi served as Prime Minister three times and became a formidable force in Italian politics as the new millennium loomed. Though charismatic and savvy, Berlusconi's leadership was marred by personal and political controversies. His Forza Italia Party, established in 1994, quickly gained popularity by championing conservative and center-right ideologies. Despite the lessons supposedly learned by the Tangentopoli Investigations, allegations of corruption, tax fraud, and sex scandals haunted the Berlusconi regime. His media empire, built when he was a private citizen, generated conflicts of interest. At the same time, his polarizing rhetoric sparked debates about media influence, democratic norms, and the independence of the judiciary in Italy.

Nevertheless, Berlusconi's tenure as Prime Minister also saw economic reforms that aimed to meet the difficulties posed by the 1990s CE. Facing high public debt, slow economic growth, and unemployment, various reforms and structural adjustments were made to address these challenges. The modernization of the world was happening at an ever-quicker pace as a technology boom took off, and Italy was forced to acknowledge the impact of globalization on its industries and workforce. This was evident in the nation's foreign policy and its continued role within the European Union (EU), of which it had been a member since the late 1950s CE.

As the new millennium dawned, Italy was wracked by another period of political instability characterized by rapid changes in government leadership. The country grappled with immigration, social welfare reform, and well-worn regional disparities between the northern and southern halves of the peninsula. On the global stage, Italy also participated in international military operations, particularly the peacekeeping missions in the Balkans and the NATO-led coalition in Afghanistan. Italian troops remained there for a lengthy period, only leaving Afghanistan in 2021 CE.

The early years of the 21st century CE were not economically kind to the Italians. The global financial crisis of 2008 CE slammed the country's economy, bringing a recession, economic instability, and high unemployment. These obstacles were frequently addressed with austerity measures, but this was unpopular among the citizens and often led to social unrest and discontent.

On the heels of fiscal devastation, like many other Western nations in the 21st century CE, there has been a significant rise of populist and anti-establishment movements. Two such are the Five Star Movement and the League Party, bolstered by social media usage. As a nation on Europe's borders, immigration and European integration have dominated the public discourse. The recent waves of migration from the Middle East and Africa have profoundly impacted the Italian peninsula, causing demographic shifts and highlighting the existing economic inequality within the nation.

Regarding its relationship with the EU, tensions have arisen over fiscal policies, migration, and Italian sovereignty. The nation's relationship with the EU is ever-evolving, but debates on the country's future in the Union and the impact of EU policies on Italian governance continually appear. Despite the struggles, Italy has embraced digitalization and innovation, with thriving fashion, design, automotive, and tourism sectors.

In the 2020s CE, the COVID-19 pandemic unnerved Italy and the world. The country was severely affected by the virus, with many cases and fatalities, becoming Europe's epicenter of the contagion in the spring of

2020. Even as the disaster of the pandemic fades into history, it starkly highlighted the fragilities of Italy's healthcare system and its integral connection to the well-being of its populace.

The future will pose significant challenges for Italy. The high public debt, low growth rates, and persistent gap between the north and the south all threaten the health of the Italian economy. Addressing structural issues, improving competitiveness, and fostering innovation will be crucial for sustainable and realistic economic growth. Furthermore, establishing political stability will be critical moving forward after several decades of fluctuating government leadership and eye-popping scandals. Strengthening institutions, promoting transparency, and enhancing public trust in politics will be essential.

Italy faces demographic challenges like many developed nations, including an aging population and low birth rates. This directly impacts the health of social security systems and future labor markets, so implementing policies to address these issues and promote social cohesion will be vital. Lastly, though climate change impacts the entire world, Italy is particularly vulnerable as a peninsular country in a warmer climate. There is a need to address environmental challenges and foster sustainable development to ensure a healthy and safe future for Italians.

Italy has been a land of opportunity and innovation since its earliest beginnings. With a deep history and many natural gifts, the nation is renowned for excellence. Heralded for the finer things that life has to offer —be that art, culture, fashion, food, wine, or even just the view of the glittering Mediterranean—Italy continues to captivate the imaginations of millions.

As we close this intriguing exploration of the beautiful tapestry that is Italy, I thank you for joining us on this journey through time and culture. If you've found *A Brief History of Italy: Tracing the Renaissance, Unification, and the Lively Evolution of Art and Culture* enlightening and captivating, I kindly ask that you take a few moments to share your thoughts on Amazon.

Your review will help others discover the riveting story of Italy's past and offer valuable feedback for us to further improve and refine our future works. Your voice matters in the narrative of history, and I am grateful for your participation and time. Grazie mille!

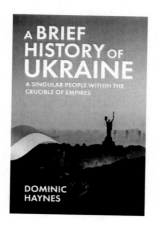

A Brief History of Ukraine: A Singular People Within the
Crucible of Empires

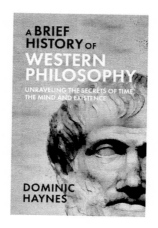

A Brief History of Western Philosophy: Unraveling the Secrets of Time, the Mind, and Existence

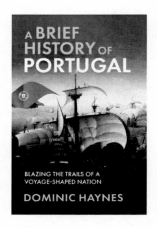

A Brief History of Portugal: Blazing the Trail of a Voyage-Shaped Nation

REFERENCES

Barzun, J., Mayne, R., Herrin, J., Stearns, P., Treasure, G., Parker, N., Peters, E., Salmon, J., Frassetto, M., Sørensen, M., Herlihy, D., Champion, T., Weinstein, D., and Aubin, H. (2023, May 22). *History of Europe. Encyclopedia Britannica.* https://www.britannica.com/topic/history-of-Europe

Berengo, M., King, R., Marino, J., et al. (2023, June 14). *Italy. Encyclopedia Britannica.* https://www.britannica.com/place/Italy

Bower, B. (2017, April 21). *Ötzi the Iceman froze to death.* Science News. https://www.sciencenews.org/article/otzi-iceman-froze-death

Brett, M., Warmington, B. and Abun-Nasr, J. (2023, June 11). *North Africa. Encyclopedia Britannica.* https://www.britannica.com/place/North-Africa

Britannica, T. Editors of Encyclopaedia. (2023, January 1). *Alfonso Ferrero La Marmora. Encyclopedia Britannica.* https://www.britannica.com/biography/Alfonso-Ferrero-La-Marmora

Britannica, T. Editors of Encyclopaedia. (2012, November 28). *Ancus Marcius. Encyclopedia Britannica.* https://www.britannica.com/topic/Ancus-Marcius

Britannica, T. Editors of Encyclopaedia. (2022, October 28). *Antonio Genovesi. Encyclopedia Britannica.* https://www.britannica.com/biography/Antonio-Genovesi

Britannica, T. Editors of Encyclopaedia. (2023, May 12). *Arianism. Encyclopedia Britannica.* https://www.britannica.com/topic/Arianism

Britannica, T. Editors of Encyclopaedia. (2022, July 18). *Avignon papacy. Encyclopedia Britannica.* https://www.britannica.com/event/Avignon-papacy

Britannica, T. Editors of Encyclopaedia. (2020, April 3). *Battle of Cynoscephalae. Encyclopedia Britannica.* https://www.britannica.com/event/Battle-of-Cynoscephalae

Britannica, T. Editors of Encyclopaedia. (2014, November 18). *Battle of Mons Lactarius. Encyclopedia Britannica.* https://www.britannica.com/event/Battle-of-Mons-Lactarius

Britannica, T. Editors of Encyclopaedia. (2019, November 6). *Battle of Pydna. Encyclopedia Britannica.* https://www.britannica.com/event/Battle-of-Pydna

Britannica, T. Editors of Encyclopaedia. (2008, July 14). *Benevento. Encyclopedia Britannica.* https://www.britannica.com/place/Benevento-Italy

Britannica, T. Editors of Encyclopaedia. (2018, March 5). *Byzantine Greek language. Encyclopedia Britannica.* https://www.britannica.com/topic/Byzantine-Greek-language

Britannica, T. Editors of Encyclopaedia. (2017, April 25). *Caesaropapism. Encyclopedia Britannica.* https://www.britannica.com/topic/caesaropapism

Britannica, T. Editors of Encyclopaedia. (2023, February 25). *Charles I. Encyclopedia Britannica.* https://www.britannica.com/biography/Charles-I-king-of-Naples-and-Sicily

Britannica, T. Editors of Encyclopaedia. (2018, April 16). *Church of San Vitale. Encyclopedia Britannica.* https://www.britannica.com/place/Church-of-San-Vitale

Britannica, T. Editors of Encyclopaedia. (1998, July 20). *Cisalpine Republic. Encyclopedia Britannica.* https://www.britannica.com/place/Cisalpine-Republic

Britannica, T. Editors of Encyclopaedia. (2023, June 26). *Clement VII. Encyclopedia Britannica.* https://www.britannica.com/biography/Clement-VII-pope

Britannica, T. Editors of Encyclopaedia. (2015, November 8). *Concordat of Worms. Encyclopedia Britannica.* https://www.britannica.com/event/Concordat-of-Worms

Britannica, T. Editors of Encyclopaedia. (2023, January 1). *Constance. Encyclopedia Britannica.* https://www.britannica.com/biography/Constance-queen-of-Sicily

Britannica, T. Editors of Encyclopaedia. (2019, July 24). *Council of Constance. Encyclopedia Britannica.* https://www.britannica.com/

event/Council-of-Constance

Britannica, T. Editors of Encyclopaedia. (2023, May 17). *Council of Trent*. *Encyclopedia Britannica*. https://www.britannica.com/event/Council-of-Trent

Britannica, T. Editors of Encyclopaedia. (2005, June 16). *Donation of Pippin*. *Encyclopedia Britannica*. https://www.britannica.com/event/Donation-of-Pippin

Britannica, T. Editors of Encyclopaedia. (2023, April 28). *Expedition of the Thousand*. *Encyclopedia Britannica*. https://www.britannica.com/event/Expedition-of-the-Thousand

Britannica, T. Editors of Encyclopaedia. (2022, November 28). *Ferdinando Galiani*. *Encyclopedia Britannica*. https://www.britannica.com/biography/Ferdinando-Galiani

Britannica, T. Editors of Encyclopaedia. (2022, October 18). *Giovanni Giolitti*. *Encyclopedia Britannica*. https://www.britannica.com/biography/Giovanni-Giolitti

Britannica, T. Editors of Encyclopaedia. (2022, June 17). *Guelf and Ghibelline*. *Encyclopedia Britannica*. https://www.britannica.com/event/Guelf-and-Ghibelline

Britannica, T. Editors of Encyclopaedia. (2018, April 1). *Haruspices*. *Encyclopedia Britannica*. https://www.britannica.com/topic/Haruspices

Britannica, T. Editors of Encyclopaedia. (2023, January 1). *Henry VI*. *Encyclopedia Britannica*. https://www.britannica.com/biography/Henry-VI-Holy-Roman-emperor

Britannica, T. Editors of Encyclopaedia. (2019, May 16). *How did Cleopatra die?*. *Encyclopedia Britannica*. https://www.britannica.com/question/How-did-Cleopatra-die

Britannica, T. Editors of Encyclopaedia. (2019, August 22). *Iron Crown of Lombardy*. *Encyclopedia Britannica*. https://www.britannica.com/topic/Iron-Crown-of-Lombardy

Britannica, T. Editors of Encyclopaedia. (2016, March 8). *Irredentist*. *Encyclopedia Britannica*. https://www.britannica.com/event/Irredentist

Britannica, T. Editors of Encyclopaedia. (2012, March 6). *Italian*

Democratic Socialist Party. Encyclopedia Britannica. https://www.britannica.com/topic/Italian-Democratic-Socialist-Party

Britannica, T. Editors of Encyclopaedia. (2023, May 2). *Italian Liberal Party. Encyclopedia Britannica.* https://www.britannica.com/topic/Italian-Liberal-Party

Britannica, T. Editors of Encyclopaedia. (2012, March 6). *Italian Popular Party. Encyclopedia Britannica.* https://www.britannica.com/topic/Italian-Popular-Party

Britannica, T. Editors of Encyclopaedia. (2023, March 6). *Kingdom of Naples. Encyclopedia Britannica.* https://www.britannica.com/place/Kingdom-of-Naples

Britannica, T. Editors of Encyclopaedia. (2015, November 11). *List of Roman emperors. Encyclopedia Britannica.* https://www.britannica.com/topic/list-of-Roman-emperors-2043294

Britannica, T. Editors of Encyclopaedia. (2019, April 17). *Lombard. Encyclopedia Britannica.* https://www.britannica.com/topic/Lombard-people

Britannica, T. Editors of Encyclopaedia. (2022, December 17). *Luigi Cadorna. Encyclopedia Britannica.* https://www.britannica.com/biography/Luigi-Cadorna

Britannica, T. Editors of Encyclopaedia. (2018, March 23). *Migration period. Encyclopedia Britannica.* https://www.britannica.com/event/Dark-Ages

Britannica, T. Editors of Encyclopaedia. (2022, December 27). *Norman. Encyclopedia Britannica.* https://www.britannica.com/topic/Norman-people

Britannica, T. Editors of Encyclopaedia. (2020, March 3). *Numa Pompilius. Encyclopedia Britannica.* https://www.britannica.com/biography/Numa-Pompilius

Britannica, T. Editors of Encyclopaedia. (2023, April 21). *Odoacer. Encyclopedia Britannica.* https://www.britannica.com/biography/Odoacer

Britannica, T. Editors of Encyclopaedia. (2018, January 25). *Oscan language. Encyclopedia Britannica.* https://www.britannica.com/topic/Oscan-language

Britannica, T. Editors of Encyclopaedia. (2023, May 15). *Pact of Steel*. *Encyclopedia Britannica*. https://www.britannica.com/event/Pact-of-Steel

Britannica, T. Editors of Encyclopaedia. (2023, January 11). *Paris Peace Conference*. *Encyclopedia Britannica*. https://www.britannica.com/event/Paris-Peace-Conference

Britannica, T. Editors of Encyclopaedia. (2011, May 3). *Pazzi conspiracy*. *Encyclopedia Britannica*. https://www.britannica.com/event/Pazzi-conspiracy

Britannica, T. Editors of Encyclopaedia. (1998, July 20). *Popolo*. *Encyclopedia Britannica*. https://www.britannica.com/topic/popolo

Britannica, T. Editors of Encyclopaedia. (2023, May 16). *Po River*. *Encyclopedia Britannica*. https://www.britannica.com/place/Po-River

Britannica, T. Editors of Encyclopaedia. (2023, January 7). *Rodolfo Graziani, marquess di Neghelli*. *Encyclopedia Britannica*. https://www.britannica.com/biography/Rodolfo-Graziani-marchese-di-Neghelli

Britannica, T. Editors of Encyclopaedia. (2023, April 25). *Roman Empire*. *Encyclopedia Britannica*. https://www.britannica.com/place/Roman-Empire

Britannica, T. Editors of Encyclopaedia. (1998, July 20). *Roman Republic*. *Encyclopedia Britannica*. https://www.britannica.com/place/Roman-Republic-historical-territory-Italy-1798-1799

Britannica, T. Editors of Encyclopaedia. (2022, May 26). *Sabine*. *Encyclopedia Britannica*. https://www.britannica.com/topic/Sabine

Britannica, T. Editors of Encyclopaedia. (2018, January 12). *Samnite*. *Encyclopedia Britannica*. https://www.britannica.com/topic/Samnite-people

Britannica, T. Editors of Encyclopaedia. (2023, June 4). *Savoy*. *Encyclopedia Britannica*. https://www.britannica.com/place/Savoy-historical-region-Europe

Britannica, T. Editors of Encyclopaedia. (2012, August 12). *Servius Tullius*. *Encyclopedia Britannica*. https://www.britannica.com/biography/Servius-Tullius

Britannica, T. Editors of Encyclopaedia. (2017, March 15). *Sforza Family*. *Encyclopedia Britannica*. https://www.britannica.com/topic/Sforza-family

Britannica, T. Editors of Encyclopaedia. (2023, March 23). *Sicilian Vespers*. *Encyclopedia Britannica*. https://www.britannica.com/event/Sicilian-Vespers

Britannica, T. Editors of Encyclopaedia. (1998, July 20). *Siege of Bari*. *Encyclopedia Britannica*. https://www.britannica.com/event/Siege-of-Bari

Britannica, T. Editors of Encyclopaedia. (2023, July 6). *Silvio Berlusconi*. *Encyclopedia Britannica*. https://www.britannica.com/biography/Silvio-Berlusconi

Britannica, T. Editors of Encyclopaedia. (2023, February 16). *Tancred*. *Encyclopedia Britannica*. https://www.britannica.com/biography/Tancred-king-of-Sicily

Britannica, T. Editors of Encyclopaedia. (2018, July 9). *Tarquin*. *Encyclopedia Britannica*. https://www.britannica.com/biography/Tarquin-king-of-Rome-616-578-BC

Britannica, T. Editors of Encyclopaedia. (2023, April 1). *Thirty Years' War*. *Encyclopedia Britannica*. https://www.britannica.com/event/Thirty-Years-War

Britannica, T. Editors of Encyclopaedia. (2022, October 10). *Treaty of Campo Formio*. *Encyclopedia Britannica*. https://www.britannica.com/event/Treaty-of-Campo-Formio

Britannica, T. Editors of Encyclopaedia. (2022, November 14). *Triple Alliance*. *Encyclopedia Britannica*. https://www.britannica.com/event/Triple-Alliance-Europe-1882-1915

Britannica, T. Editors of Encyclopaedia. (2017, March 27). *Tullus Hostilius*. *Encyclopedia Britannica*. https://www.britannica.com/biography/Tullus-Hostilius

Britannica, T. Editors of Encyclopaedia. (2016, May 2). *Umbri*. *Encyclopedia Britannica*. https://www.britannica.com/topic/Umbri

Britannica, T. Editors of Encyclopaedia. (2023, February 17). *Venetia*. *Encyclopedia Britannica*. https://www.britannica.com/place/Venetia

Britannica, T. Editors of Encyclopaedia. (2023, March 10). *Victor*

Emmanuel II. Encyclopedia Britannica. https://www.britannica.com/biography/Victor-Emmanuel-II

Britannica, T. Editors of Encyclopaedia. (2018, August 1). *Villanovan culture. Encyclopedia Britannica.* https://www.britannica.com/topic/Villanovan-culture

Britannica, T. Editors of Encyclopaedia. (2002, June 14). *Visconti Family. Encyclopedia Britannica.* https://www.britannica.com/topic/Visconti-family

Britannica, T. Editors of Encyclopaedia. (2022, May 11). *Vitruvius. Encyclopedia Britannica.* https://www.britannica.com/biography/Vitruvius

Britannica, T. Editors of Encyclopaedia. (2023, May 23). *War of the Spanish Succession. Encyclopedia Britannica.* https://www.britannica.com/event/War-of-the-Spanish-Succession

Britannica, T. Editors of Encyclopaedia. (2023, April 5). *Zeno. Encyclopedia Britannica.* https://www.britannica.com/biography/Zeno-emperor

Broers, M. (2001, July). Noble Romans and Regenerated Citizens: The Morality of Conscription in Napoleonic Italy, 1800–1814. *War in History, 8*(3), 249–270. https://www.jstor.org/stable/26013945

Bunting, T. (2023, April 29). *Sack of Rome. Encyclopedia Britannica.* https://www.britannica.com/event/Sack-of-Rome-1527

Callihan, K. (2020, April 5). *The Mysterious Nuragic Civilization of Sardinia.* Ancient Origins. https://www.ancient-origins.net/history-ancient-traditions/nuragic-sardinia-004841

Capelli, C., Onofri, V., Brisighelli, F., et al. (2009, January 21). Moors and Saracens in Europe: Estimating the medieval North African male legacy in southern Europe. *European Journal of Human Genetics, 17*(6), 848–852. 10.1038/ejhg.2008.258

Cartwright, M. (2017, March 3). *Lucius Tarquinius Superbus.* World History Encyclopedia. https://www.worldhistory.org/Lucius_Tarquinius_Superbus/

Cartwright, M. (2017, February 6). *Villanovan Culture.* World History Encyclopedia. https://www.worldhistory.org/Villanovan_Culture/

Chakra, H. (2021, August 28). *History of the Emirate of Sicily.* About

History. https://about-history.com/history-of-the-emirate-of-sicily/

Chisholm, H. (1911). *Tarquinius Priscus, Lucius. In* Chisholm (ed.), *Encyclopaedia Britannica* (11th edition). Cambridge University Press.

Civic Museums of Reggio Emilia. (n.d.). *The First Metal: The discovery of the Copper Age site of Remedello.* Google Arts & Culture. https://artsandculture.google.com/story/the-first-metal-musei-civici-di-reggio-emilia/KgXRxN5_c2eUKg?hl=en

Claus, P. (2022, July 25). *How Ancient Greece Shaped the Thought of Dante.* Greek Reporter. https://greekreporter.com/2022/07/25/how-ancient-greece-shaped-thought-dante

Costelloe, T. (2022, September 15). *Giambattista Vico.* Stanford Encyclopedia of Philosophy. https://plato.stanford.edu/entries/vico/

Cousin, J. (2023, May 6). *Diocletian. Encyclopedia Britannica.* https://www.britannica.com/biography/Diocletian

Davis, D. [Dan Davis History]. (2021, December 23). *The Terramare Culture and the Bronze Age Collapse* [Video]. YouTube. https://www.youtube.com/watch?v=oL5GDXq1acE&list=TLPQMDQwNjIwMjOW5rXdvViyNQ&index=1&ab_channel=DanDavisHistory

Dante, A. (2012, January 20). *Erano padani i primi abitanti d'Italia (Translated: The first inhabitants of Italy were in the Po Valley.* National Geographic Italia. http://www.nationalgeographic.it/scienza/2012/01/20/news/erano_padani_iprimi_abitanti_ditalia-807204/

Da Vinci—The Renaissance Man. (n.d.). Museum of Science, Boston. https://www.mos.org/leonardo/biography

Duomo Florence Cathedral. (n.d.). Florence Museum. https://www.florence-museum.com/duomo-florence-cathedral-santa-maria-del-fiore.php

Editorial Staff. (2011, March 10). *The Italian Risorgimento: A timeline.* The Florentine. https://www.theflorentine.net/2011/03/10/the-italian-risorgimento-a-timeline/

Egypt Today Staff. (2017, June 1). *Muslim Sicily: The Rise and Fall of Islam in Italy.* Egypt Today. https://www.egypttoday.com/Article/4/6246/Muslim-Sicily-The-rise-and-fall-of-Islam-in-Italy

Ferdinandy, M. de. (2023, June 20). *Charles V. Encyclopedia Britannica.* https://www.britannica.com/biography/Charles-V-Holy-Roman-emperor

Fife, S. (2012, January 18). *The Brothers Gracchi: The Tribunates of Tiberius and Gaius Gracchus.* World History Encyclopedia. https://www.worldhistory.org/article/95/the-brothers-gracchi-the-tribunates-of-tiberius--g/

Fleming, W., Millon, H., Cannon-Brookes, P., et al. (2023, June 1). *Western architecture. Encyclopedia Britannica.* https://www.britannica.com/art/Western-architecture

Foot, J. and Lecco, A. (2023, June 19). *Milan. Encyclopedia Britannica.* https://www.britannica.com/place/Milan-Italy

Foot, J., Cessi, R., and Cosgrove, D. (2023, June 1). *Venice. Encyclopedia Britannica.* https://www.britannica.com/place/Venice

Frothingham, A. (1917). Vediovis, the Volcanic God: A Reconstruction. *The American Journal of Philology, 38*(4), 370–391. https://doi.org/10.2307/288964

Garcia, B. (2018, April 18). *Romulus and Remus.* World History Encyclopedia. https://www.worldhistory.org/Romulus_and_Remus/

Gilbert, A. (2023, June 7). *Battle of Marengo. Encyclopedia Britannica.* https://www.britannica.com/event/Battle-of-Marengo

Gillett, A. (2001). Rome, Ravenna and the Last Western Emperors. *Papers of the British School at Rome, 69,* 131–167. http://www.jstor.org/stable/40311008

Goodwin, A., and Popkin, J. (2023, June 30). *Louis XVI. Encyclopedia Britannica.* https://www.britannica.com/biography/Louis-XVI

Grab, A. (2008, April 25). The politics of finance in Napoleonic Italy (1802–1814). *Journal of Modern Italian Studies, 3*(2), 127–143. https://doi.org/10.1080/13545719808454972

Hart, B. (2023, May 6). *North Africa campaigns. Encyclopedia Britannica.* https://www.britannica.com/event/North-Africa-campaigns

Hibbert, C., and Foot, John. (2023, June 16). *Benito Mussolini. Encyclopedia Britannica.* https://www.britannica.com/biography/Benito-Mussolini

Hicks, P. (n.d.). *How Napoleon Became 'King of Italy'.* Napoleon. https://www.napoleon.org/en/history-of-the-two-empires/articles/how-napoleon-became-king-of-italy/

History.com Editors. (2022, January 7). *Erwin Rommel.* History. https://www.history.com/topics/world-war-ii/erwin-rommel

History.com Editors. (2023, April 20). *Renaissance.* History. https://www.history.com/topics/renaissance/renaissance

Hudson, M. (2019, September 11). *Battle of Pharsalus. Encyclopedia Britannica.* https://www.britannica.com/event/Battle-of-Pharsalus

Inturrisi, L. (1987, April 26). Tracing The Norman Rulers of Sicily. *The New York Times.* https://www.nytimes.com/1987/04/26/travel/tracing-the-norman-rulers-of-sicily.html

Irwin, D. (2023, April 3). *Neoclassical art. Encyclopedia Britannica.* https://www.britannica.com/art/Neoclassicism

Italy, 500 CE. (n.d.). Time Maps. https://timemaps.com/history/italy-500ad/

Italian Peninsula, 1000 B.C.–1 A.D. (n.d.). The Metropolitan Museum of Art. https://www.metmuseum.org/toah/ht/04/eust.html

Kertzer, D. (n.d.). *Projects: The Rise and Fall of the Roman Republic.* Brown University. https://watson.brown.edu/research/projects/roman_republic

Khan, S. (2020, May 14). *Frederick II.* World History Encyclopedia. https://www.worldhistory.org/Frederick_II/

Kindy, D. (2021, September 29). *Where Did the Ancient Etruscans Come From?* The Smithsonian Magazine. https://www.smithsonianmag.com/smart-news/dna-analysis-shows-early-etruscans-were-homegrown-180978772/

King, G. (2008). *The Development of Free Trade in Europe.* Hillsdale College. https://www.hillsdale.edu/educational-outreach/free-market-forum/2008-archive/the-development-of-free-trade-in-europe/

Lee, T. (2014, August 19). *40 maps that explain the Roman Empire.* Vox Media. https://www.vox.com/world/2018/6/19/17469176/roman-empire-maps-history-explained

Little, B. (2022, March 3). *How Regional Conflicts Snowballed into World*

War I. History. https://www.history.com/news/regional-conflict-world-war-i-beginning

Lynch, J. (2023, March 29). *Charles III. Encyclopedia Britannica.* https://www.britannica.com/biography/Charles-III-king-of-Spain

Mapping Militant Organizations. (2018, June). *Red Brigades.* Stanford University. https://cisac.fsi.stanford.edu/mappingmilitants/profiles/red-brigades

Marcelli, U. (2023, June 2). *Camillo Benso, count di Cavour. Encyclopedia Britannica.* https://www.britannica.com/biography/Camillo-Benso-conte-di-Cavour

Mark, H. (2023, May 10). *Battle of Rivoli.* World History Encyclopedia. https://www.worldhistory.org/article/2234/battle-of-rivoli/

Mark, J. (2019, September 20). *Belisarius.* World History Encyclopedia. https://www.worldhistory.org/Belisarius/

Mark, J. (2009, September 2). *Sea Peoples.* World History Encyclopedia. https://www.worldhistory.org/Sea_Peoples/

Mark, J. (2014, October 9). *Theodoric the Great.* World History Encyclopedia. https://www.worldhistory.org/Theodoric_the_Great/

Mark, J. (2022, August 11). *Thirty Years' War.* World History Encyclopedia. https://www.worldhistory.org/Thirty_Years'_War/

Martini, M., Simonetti, O., Orsini, D., et al. (2022, January 31). The avid eaters of lives. New and old infectious diseases in Italy at the time of World War I: a historical overview of military medicine and public health. *Journal of Preventative Medicine and Hygiene, 62*(4): E972–E980. 10.15167/2421-4248/jpmh2021.62.4.2240

Mattozzi, S. (2019, May 13). *Sicilians have affinity for the Islamic world in their DNA.* Al Jazeera. https://www.aljazeera.com/features/2019/5/13/sicilians-have-affinity-for-the-islamic-world-in-their-dna

Murray, P. J. (2023, January 4). *Giotto. Encyclopedia Britannica.* https://www.britannica.com/biography/Giotto-di-Bondone

Netchev, S. (2022, September 9). *Charlemagne and the Carolingian Empire, c. 814.* World History Encyclopedia. https://www.worldhistory.org/image/16359/charlemagne-and-the-carolingian-empire-c-814/

Palma, G., Wickham, C., Signoretta, P., et al. (2023, June 10). *Italy.* *Encyclopedia Britannica.* https://www.britannica.com/place/Italy

Peretto, C. (2006). The first peopling of southern Europe: The Italian case. *Comptes Rendus Palevol, 5*(1–2), 283–290. https://doi.org/10.1016/j.crpv.2005.11.006

Pick, R. (2023, May 9). *Maria Theresa. Encyclopedia Britannica.* https://www.britannica.com/biography/Maria-Theresa

Pohl, F. (2023, May 19). *Tiberius. Encyclopedia Britannica.* https://www.britannica.com/biography/Tiberius

Popham, P. (2008, June 19). *Return of Dante: The Guelphs and the Ghibellines.* The Independent. https://www.independent.co.uk/news/world/europe/return-of-dante-the-guelphs-and-the-ghibellines-850012.html

Rich, N. (2005, August 21). Misunderstood southern Italy. *The Los Angeles Times.* https://www.latimes.com/archives/la-xpm-2005-aug-21-bk-rich21-story.html

Rome Timeline. (n.d.). World History Encyclopedia. https://www.worldhistory.org/timeline/Rome/

Samnite Timeline. (n.d.). World History Encyclopedia. https://www.worldhistory.org/timeline/samnite/

Sandbrook, D. (2021, September 18). *The death of Domitian: how Roman aristocrats conspired against the emperor.* History Extra. https://www.historyextra.com/period/roman/18-september-ad-96-domitian-is-stabbed/

Serafin, C. (2021, November 26). *Roman Warfare in the Age of Pyrrhus.* World History Encyclopedia. https://www.worldhistory.org/article/1881/roman-warfare-in-the-age-of-pyrrhus/

Smith, W. (2022, September 16). *Flag of Italy. Encyclopedia Britannica.* https://www.britannica.com/topic/flag-of-Italy

Starnini, E., Biagi, P., and Mazzucco, N. (2018, March 20). The beginning of the Neolithic in the Po Plain (northern Italy): Problems and Perspectives. *Quaternary International, 470*(B), 301–317. https://doi.org/10.1016/j.quaint.2017.05.059

Sullivan, R. E. (2023, May 15). *Charlemagne. Encyclopedia Britannica.* https://www.britannica.com/biography/Charlemagne

Taglibue, J. (2000, January 20). Bettino Craxi, Italian Prime Minister Who Was Tainted By Corruption, Dies at 65. *The New York Times*. https://www.nytimes.com/2000/01/20/world/bettino-craxi-italian-prime-minister-who-was-tainted-by-corruption-dies-at-65.html

The Iceman. (n.d.). South Tyrol Museum of Archaeology. https://www.iceman.it/en/the-iceman/

The Roman Empire: A Brief History. (n.d.). Milwaukee Public Museum. https://www.mpm.edu/research-collections/anthropology/anthropology-collections-research/mediterranean-oil-lamps/roman-empire-brief-history

Thomson, R. (2019, February 4). *The birthplace of modern medicine*. BBC. https://www.bbc.com/travel/article/20190203-the-birthplace-of-modern-medicine

Varriale, A. (2021, June 8). *Institutionalized Populism: The "Strange Case" of the Italian Five Star Movement*. European Center for Populism Studies. https://www.populismstudies.org/institutionalized-populism-the-strange-case-of-the-italian-five-star-movement/

Wakefield, A. (2022, October 17). *Battle of Vittorio Veneto. Encyclopedia Britannica*. https://www.britannica.com/topic/Battle-of-Vittorio-Veneto

Watts, E. (2021, October 6). Rome Didn't Fall When You Think It Did. Here's Why That Fabricated History Still Matters Today. *Time Magazine*. https://time.com/6101964/fabricated-fall-rome-lessons-history/

Wills, M. (2022, October 28). *Mussolini's Colonial Inspiration*. JSTOR Daily. https://daily.jstor.org/mussolinis-colonial-inspiration/

Winfield, N. (2020, December 16). *A pandemic atlas: Italy becomes Europe's viral epicenter*. Associated Press. https://apnews.com/article/pandemics-europe-italy-health-coronavirus-pandemic-f71955b0327aa9f7a0c2e44b9f485475

Made in United States
North Haven, CT
19 December 2024

62908810R00109